Facets of
Arab
Nationalism

Facets of Arab Nationalism

by Hans E. Tütsch

Wayne State University Press, Detroit, 1965

Waynebook No. 16

To Brida, *who has shared the pains and pleasures of years of traveling* *with her journalist husband.*

Contents

Preface / 9

1. *The Impact of Western Civilization* / 11

2. *Arab Unity—Islamic Unity* / 29

    A. Four Elements of Arab Unity / 31

        1. RELIGION / 2. LANGUAGE / 3. LAW / 4. HISTORY

    B. The Bonds of Islam / 47

        1. UNIVERSALISM / 2. RELIGIOUS AND SECULAR NATIONALISM / 3. MUTA-
TIONS OF NATIONALISM / 4. PAN-ISLAMISM / 5. ISLAMIC PARTIES / 6.
CHRISTIANS AND MUSLIMS / 7. AN ISLAMIC REFORMATION?

3. *The Quest for Unity* / 75

    A. Pan-Arab Nationalism / 77

    B. The League of Arab States / 87

    C. Nasserism / 90

    D. Arab Versions of Socialism / 98

4. *Arab Dissensions* / 107

    A. Secularism—A Centrifugal Force / 109

    B. Local Nationalism / 116

Contents

    C. *Regional Nationalism* / 124

    D. *Arab Imperialism* / 128

    E. *Arab Nationalism versus Israel* / 132

    F. *Nationalism and Communism* / 133

Notes / 139

Bibliography / 147

Index / 153

Preface

      Facets of Arab Nationalism is an attempt to present a synthesis of my impressions of the Arab world. My information has been gathered in the years since 1955 on many trips through North Africa and the Middle East while working as a foreign correspondent for the *Neue Zürcher Zeitung*. During my travels I have personally met a great number of the intellectual and political leaders from Morocco to Kuwait.

      The main body of the book was written while I was Visiting Professor of History at Wayne State University, Detroit. The final draft was concluded August 1, 1964, and events after that date have not been included in this account of the Arab world. I have rendered the Arabic words in a simplified form as used by newspapers. The citations, however, are given unchanged, even if divergences in spelling result. Translations of foreign language quotations into English are mine where not otherwise noted. All opinions are my own and are not to be attributed to either the *Neue Zürcher Zeitung* or Wayne State University.

      The various forms of Arab nationalism and the impact of Western civilization on Arab society are the main concern of *Facets of Arab Nationalism*. Western technology may well be on the way toward becoming universal, but as Raymond Aron says: "Long after the world has been united by technology, men will continue to believe in rival gods."

Hans E. Tütsch
Zürich, Switzerland

1. The Impact of Western Civilization

What does this sudden uneasiness mean,
and this confusion? (How grave the faces have become!)
Why are the streets and squares rapidly emptying,
and why is everyone going back home so lost in thought?

Because it is night and the barbarians have not come.
And some men have arrived from the frontiers
and they say that there are no barbarians any longer.

And now, what will become of us without barbarians?
Those people were a kind of solution.

C. P. Cavafy, "Waiting for the Barbarians,"
in *Six Poets of Modern Greece.* Translated
by Edmund Keeley and Philip Sherrard
(New York: Alfred A. Knopf, Inc., 1961).

"There are no barbarians any longer. And now, what will become of us without barbarians? Those people were a kind of solution." So chants the Greek poet Cavafy (Cavafis) in Lawrence Durrell's pre-Nasserian Alexandria. No barbarians any more; indeed, never have the barriers between civilizations been lowered to such a degree since Hellenistic times. Immense forces batter down the tight compartments in which civilizations were enclosed, and only the Communist machine of coercion preserves some prison walls unbreached. Nobody is called deaf and dumb (*ajam*, or, in Slavic languages, *nemec*) because he uses a different tongue, nobody set apart as a barbarian because he does not share in the same culture. The globe may not be subdivided any more in separate "universes"—the Roman and the Chinese "universal" empires, the Christian and Islamic realms—as it was until recent times, but still we speak of "worlds," the Communist world, the Arab world where barricades, spiritual or political, persist. Domination of all five continents by Europeans, or people of European origin, in the first half of the twentieth century spread Western civilization over the whole earth. Western technology has opened up access to hidden corners and has conquered regions once so remote that ancient maps had written on white spaces: *Hic sunt leones.* Now, where the lions roamed, delegates prepare for their trip to the United Nations.

Montaigne[1] asserts: "Everyone gives the title of barbarism to everything that is not according to his usage; as, indeed, we have no other criterion of truth and reason than the example and pattern of the opinions and customs of the country wherein we live. There always is the perfect religion, there the perfect government, there the perfect and accomplished usage in all things. They are savages in the same way that we say fruits are wild, which nature produces of herself and by her ordinary course; whereas, in truth, we ought rather to call those wild, whose natures we have changed by our artifice, and diverted from the common order." Other criterions of truth and reason have been established in the last two hundred years in place of parochial comparisons but still Montaigne's nationalism *avant la lettre* survives. Hardly anything or anyone has escaped changes by our artifice and has not been diverted from an old-established common order and brought into the new *ecumenicity* of technology.

Technology, Western culture's material offspring, prevails in the vast process of acculturation which grips the world. Spiritual unity or a political "one world," on the other hand, still seem far away. There is, however, another element of order deep-rooted in the spiritual, but as highly formalized as though sprung from technological spheres, which has conquered large segments of the present world, and that element is Western law. The application of European law, be it Germanic or Roman in origin, in far away Africa and Asia may sometimes appear as a travesty, but does it not channel thought and action, custom and belief in a direction outlined by Western culture?

Mystical thinking in Germanic lands expects salvation from the East. The East, however, expects salvation from the West and violently vents its disappointment when revelation arrives not on wings of phantasy but with the unspiritual noise of running motors. But for some, like the thirty-year old Damascene poet Elias al-Fadel, "the sun arises in the West."

The Arab world, united by Muhammad and the creed revealed through him, brought to an end a thousand years of "Western" culture around the Mediterranean Sea, a culture created by the Greeks, transmitted by Alexander of Macedonia, inherited by Rome, infused with Hebrew monotheistic belief, and transformed by Christianity. Islam may be considered as a simple heresy[2] or "immediately intelligible to the Christian,"[3] and certainly it has absorbed much of the ancient heritage of the Mediterranean world. But to Muslims and Christians alike it was and still is felt as something different, completely alien, developing in its own frame of reference and creating special modes of thought and action.[4]

The religious conflicts and armed battles were as real and as deeply felt as a certain community of ideas established around the Mediterranean area since ancient times. A Westerner talking with an Arab is struck by their two divergent lines of thought, while with a Turk or Berber a European may more easily find common ground. The difference is evidenced most strikingly by a comparison of two Algerian writers of high value, Kateb Yacine,[5] the Arab, and Mouloud Feraoun,[6] the Berber. While Feraoun thinks linearly, Yacine proceeds in spirals.

The different patterns of thought are revealed clearly in the approach toward modern technology, which is entirely a Western technology. Practically all the important inventions of the last six centuries have been made in the relatively small area which comprises Europe, from the Urals to the Atlantic Ocean, and North America. Modern technology bridges the gaps between different cultures and tends to create a single civilization, while it transforms older cultures and changes their bearers. Many, however, become members of the new civilization with only one part of their mind, while the rest of their personality remains dominated by older customs and forms of thinking.

Han Suyin expresses this duplicity of Western and Eastern

personality and the switches from one to another nicely: "These switches from one layer of personal expression to another happen often among us Asians. We have undergone so much revolution within ourselves, as well as in our externals, during the past few decades that we are able to encompass a range of several centuries of behavior and platitudes and rituals of social exchange, depending upon the situations we confront. We have become as stratified as onions in eras of time and layers of culture."[7]

Characteristic of the Arab world are not only the different layers of thought but the fact that Arabs simultaneously accept and reject Western civilization, contemporaneously admire and negate their own past which they oppose to Western culture. The Arabs are haunted by their history. Their ancestors make them feel guilty when the accomplishments of the last seven centuries are compared with the achievements in the first two or three centuries after Muhammad. And many Arab nationalists project their present difficulties unto others and hold Turks and West Europeans, and neo-colonialists, feudalists, and capitalists responsible for their own failures.

At the same time the introduction of products of Western civilization seems to increase in a geometrical proportion. The Arabs want to appropriate Western technology and its accompanying higher living standards, and they participate in the explosive enlargement of each man's horizon due to new knowledge. A desire to acquire a modern education permeates the Arab world and imposes itself on sometimes rather hesitant governments. Nothing is considered more a sign of a reactionary spirit than reluctance to provide a universal Western-type education. But where barriers to understanding arise or persist, violent emotional reactions often break forth which may take hold of a whole nation. The personalizing of issues may lead to such aggressiveness that one is tempted to assume that juvenile delinquency is not restricted to individuals but may attack whole nations.

When walking through the bazaars of Fez and Rabat, of

Tunis and Tripoli, of Cairo and Beirut, of Damascus and Aleppo, of Baghdad and Kuwait, forget for a while any previously read romantic descriptions and observe the markets with unprejudiced eyes. You will see that the bazaar has lost, or is losing, one of its two basic functions. The bazaars are no longer production centers but strictly distribution places, horizontally organized like shopping centers in the United States, for example the famous Northland of Detroit. Where once artisans sat beside traders, or the same man produced and sold his wares, as in the medieval European city, now manufacturing has been reduced to a minimum, and the local goods are often shoddy. Western products have displaced the indigenous handicrafts. In some corner a few artisans, the last of their trade, reproduce inlaid tables, copper plates, and leather purses according to old and artistically fine models; the rest of the bazaar concentrates on selling mass-produced imports. The only exception, to our knowledge, is the bazaar of Marrakesh. Fez, on the other hand, may serve as the typical example of the displacement of manufacturing by trade in Western goods; from one day to the next, one sees old workshops disappear and their successors display Western products.

Damascus, once world famous for its handicrafts, has not produced Damascene steel since Tamerlane's army sacked the city; Damascene glass, shown in every museum of Islamic arts, has been manufactured in Bohemia for the last two centuries. Damask is now unknown in Damascus; brocade is still produced on half a dozen looms, displayed for foreigners, but most of what is shown in the bazaar has been brought in from Japan and Germany. Arab copper plates come from India, the little coffee cups from Germany or Japan. Shepherds come and buy plastic overcoats from Europe, and nylon underwear from the United States attracts the ladies.

The streets of Beirut used to display a colorful spectacle of oriental costumes, men in fez and baggy pants, women veiled, many in the imaginative dress of their tribe or region. All of this is disappearing with incredible speed. Blue jeans are preferred by youths who drink Cokes or Pepsi-Colas while their elders sip their whiskey. Bob Azzam becomes world famous and a superstar in the Middle East for his jazz, and the Twist appeals to the younger generation more than traditional songs and dances. The national anthem resounds in Western tones. The armies parade with Western European, Russian, or American arms. From guns to jets, from nails to atom reactor, everything is imported from one of the four manufacturing centers of the world: Western Europe, Russia, North America, and Japan. The Asian Arabs who have done without the wheel for transportation, now jump all intermediate stages of cart, bicycle, and railroad and avail themselves with the greatest naturalness of Cadillacs and jet planes. The West may have borrowed from the East—motels are horizontally organized like caravanserais, *loukum* antecedes chewing gum, strip tease corresponds to oriental customs—but everything returns now, transformed into Western shape. Radio and television send information to the hidden corners of the desert; Bedouins listen to the news in their tents—cunning agitators give them free batteries or transistors. There are no "hicks" and "rubes," no uninformed backwoodsmen any more. All men now develop the same high expectancies, and this is political dynamite.

The transition from expecting the good things of modern technology to acquiring them by one's own work seems hard for many in the Arab world to accept. Capital has to be invested for long terms, work organized along modern lines, know-how acquired in schools or through apprenticeships, markets for the goods must be found; all this requires a profound change in basic attitudes. In the Arab world, the entrepreneur is most likely a Christian or a foreigner.

In Lebanon, where capital is not lacking, where labor is plentiful, where illiteracy has all but disappeared, where four universities provide modern education, hardly any native industry has been created—a Swiss-owned cement factory is still the biggest employer. The shrewd traders and bankers of the Levant shy away from long term investment in production. They prefer business from man to man, where a word replaces a contract. The exchange of goods from hand to hand makes complicated correspondence superfluous.

But in a modern economy one must take risks, and haggling is a loss of time. Already in southern Europe contracts are so complicated that they express insecurity and mutual distrust more than a desire to conclude business. This is even more apparent in the Arab world. The state, furthermore, drives producers into partial concealment and mendacity, where the number of employees and the production figures are hidden, and a system of triple accounting—one set of books for the tax collector, one for the shareholders or associates, and one for the head of the company—is used. The biggest "industry" in the Arab world remains speculation in real estate.

The special ethos necessary to produce is still lacking in most parts of the Mediterranean area—not solely in the Arab countries. To dirty one's hands is degrading. Therefore, one studies law rather than agriculture, one becomes an engineer, not a technician, and one deserts the land when drought strikes or when funds can be accumulated. Young men feel like Studs Lonigan: "He didn't mind work, he guessed. It was the looking for it, having to learn things about it and seeming like a goof while he was learning." To learn, to make mistakes, to be taught—these seem somehow dishonorable to Mediterranean man; he feels himself born a master —and remains as often as not a more or less gifted dilettante.

Abbé Sieyès, leading voice of the French Revolution, decried such a state of affairs: "What a society, in which work is said to derogate, where it is honorable to consume but humiliating to produce, where the laborious occupations are called vile, as if anything were vile except vice, or as if the classes that work were the most vicious!"[8] What is missing in the Arab world are a Cincinnatus or at least *Georgica*, a praise of labor, of work in connection with nature, of creating. What is missing, furthermore, is *homo faber,* man the inventor seeking redemption by his work, from do-it-yourself man to genius. Not Dr. Faust, not even Dudintsev's inventor, could be at home in the Arab world. Even Jacques Berque, who lovingly seeks out Arab solutions and approaches to problems created by the impact of Western technology, can find few inventors there.[9] If an inventor appears it will take a long time before he, as a man who dirties his hands, acquires status. The social "climate" is not yet favorable to experiments, to the trial and error which lead to inventions.

Production, the imitative introduction of foreign processes for manufacturing, can be dissociated from the spiritual background against which the methods were developed. But not for long. A fleet of jet planes, an oil refinery, and a nuclear reactor are status symbols which no underdeveloped country will do without. It is not too difficult to produce what others have produced before. But to invent is something else again. The gap between Western and Eastern civilization can be bridged temporarily by borrowing techniques, capital, and advisors, but it will reopen as soon as new inventions reshape technology. An Eastern inventor, an exception, if he remains in the East is deprived of any social significance as long as his accomplishment does not take root in any fertile soil of general receptiveness to just such innovations.

Young engineers emigrate to Europe or America to find an atmosphere more favorable to their initiative. Muhammad Ali's industries, established after Napoleon's invasion, at the time when Europe and America were embarking on the Industrial Revolution, withered on the vine. Even modern Turkey's industries just manage to stumble along. The easy way out of the dilemma is to import and pay with money gained from oil royalties or Suez Canal fees. Even canned food is brought in from the West to the Near and Middle East, where local fresh produce abounds.

The first group to take possession of modern technology and, based on this superior knowledge, form a new class aspiring to dominate the nation, are the military officers. Their use of modern technology by definition remains unproductive, it is consumption in a wider sense. Officers have been trained in foreign countries or at home by foreign instructors in a foreign language. They acquire a special skill in handling foreign arms. Their alienation from the mainstream of society is all too obvious, and it breeds impatience with the retardation of their fellow citizens and the alleged or real corruption and sluggishness of political leaders. It creates resentment against the military superiority of Westerners. As the Turkish conquest of the Arab countries in the sixteenth century was founded on superior military techniques, so European domination of the Arab world was the result of technological supremacy. While Arab countries have to buy their heavy armament and often even guns and ammunition abroad, the Western powers and Russia threaten each other with instant extinction, due to their inventions of rockets and hydrogen bombs. Not a desirable progress, certainly, but still an advance that leaves all others farther in arrears than they ever were and diminishes their field of independent action.

Colonial powers created a framework of communications and initiated the first steps toward industrialization, and they introduced a modern system of education in place of unprogressive religious schools. Better communications and a centralized administration prepared the ground for nationalism, which found an ideal breeding ground in Western schools. "Uncolonized" countries like Liberia, Ethiopia, Yemen, and even Greece and Turkey, until recent times have remained partially or totally the most backward of their area. But observing how an infinitesimal group of European soldiers and bureaucrats, often not representative of the highest standards of their country, administered vast empires, the subjugated populations, or at least their elite, assumed they could accomplish the same feat that foreigners had, just as Lenin proclaimed 16,000 Bolsheviks could govern Russia as well as the 16,000 landowners who decided Moscow's fate. These peoples crave self-assertion and refuse to remain "human accessories to the oil wells."

"Our Western know-how has unified the whole world . . . and it has inflamed the institutions of War and Class, which are the two congenital diseases of civilization, into utterly fatal maladies," opines Arnold J. Toynbee.[10] But the participation in this know-how is still most unequal, even where access to it has been opened decades ago. Furthermore, this know-how has been grafted on spiritual and social structures to which it is alien. Know-how is not enough to bridge the abyss which still divides the developed and underdeveloped countries and which tends in many areas to become deeper, not smaller. "The gigantic forms of monolithic social integration favored by technology"[11] have first crushed most of the ancient social structures in the Arab world. Men are thrown into a vortex of uncertainties created by the impact of Western economic and technological superiority. The old guilds dissolve; they will be supplanted by trade unions, which for the time being are still largely political instruments, not organizations that provide better conditions for the workers. Instead of family or tribal assistance, one gets social security, which lacks the warmth of human contact. The tribal organization is supplanted by co-operatives in the countryside, while in cities the neighborhood becomes the basis of a social and political unit.

In the civil war of 1958 in Beirut and other Lebanese cities, neighborhoods became the nuclei of political and military action; they closed themselves off by barricades and fought the "enemy" in the next block. In a similar way nationalists and Communists separated themselves from each other in Iraq in the troubled first two years of Abdul Karim Kassem's regime.

The Arab city is always full of tensions. Its function, as Ibn Khaldun pointed out, is to satisfy the human desire for luxury, refinement, and leisure. It is the scene of the historical cycle of the irruption of unspoiled peoples from the steppes and deserts, of a cultural and economic rise, and through degeneration and corruption, to the final ruin. The Arab city, therefore, appears not primarily as market place and fortress as in Europe; it is not the socio-political unit of the Greek *polis,* but it is a gathering place of consumers, a center of the leisure class, conspicuous consumption, and status seeking. Its class contrasts are more evident than anywhere in the West.

The old conflict between pashas and effendis[12] has given way to more deadly struggles. Not only the sons and grandsons of the effendis of yesteryear but also descendants of the serfs and semi-serfs are lifting their heads. The ancient pluralistic society with its tight compartments is battered down. Masses in a sociological sense are formed. Only the religious communities, frozen in the *millets* of Arab-Turkish law, resist the change. Under this system, all matters of personal status—marriage, divorce, burial, and some aspects of inheritance—are subject to the exclusive jurisdiction of religious courts.

Social and economic disunity and inequity remain flagrant. Social and economic development are closely interrelated to technological advancement; if one is out of step, the others are retarded. Between the liberty of the city and the tribal freedom of the Bedouin there still extends a broad zone of non-liberty in which the fellahin are entangled. Their emancipation has just begun, they are not yet fully integrated in the nation.

The Arab world is undoubtedly in the grip of "telescoped revolutions." It suffers the torturous pains of Renaissance and Reformation; of Enlightenment; of liberalism, propounded mainly by the merchant class; and of socialism, advocated by an intelligentsia who, believing the state could generate more initiative than individuals, woo the people. Nationalism and communism offer easy solutions for difficult problems; tribalism and agrarian dependence on local chiefs and absentee landowners have to be fought and industrialization begun. Urbanization and "population explosion" create new tasks. The principle of political organization by law and territory instead of kinship and personal rule must be established; centralization of power and development of national consciousness go hand in hand. While Western man is in the turmoil

of Ernesto Grassi's "second Enlightenment" and the second technological revolution, the Arabs are just starting with the first. While
Westerners worry about the development of C. P. Snow's "two
cultures"—the separation of technological from humanistic thought
—Arabs come up against alien spiritual frames of reference. These
"telescoped revolutions" offer an enormous challenge—but contain the risk of failure. If the secret of Europe is to be found in its
modern science and technology which is "essentially different and
without parallel in Asia," according to Karl Jaspers, then to pene-
trate it, one has to reach far down to its spiritual roots. "Technology
does not belong to the epidermis of European culture, but is nur-
tured on its very lifeblood and its most spiritual aspirations, and
has so developed that it pervades and conditions all, and being
in its mature form an easily appropriable instrument, it takes with
it, even if only obliquely and implicitly, the most varied impulses,
values, and ideals of European life."[13]

It is often lamented that the Arabs acquire from the West only
the material products of its civilization. This is only partially true.
The reception of Western law exerts an impact on the population
which is at least comparable to Western technology, even if it is
optically less effective. Courts of law must solve a wide variety of
social, economic, and political problems. They do so in the Arab
countries according to rules much less influenced by Islam than by
the principles of Roman and Germanic law, Greek philosophy,
Hebrew and Christian ethics. The exception to this is in the
Arabian Peninsula and in more modern states, small sectors of the
law of persons. In general, the bureaucracy administers according
to European regulations, rather than to Islamic customs.

Western-type institutions in some instances are given a new
content, and the system of command does not always correspond
to the system of law. But nevertheless these institutions change the
way of life of the population. They become instruments of social
change; a change, it is true, which is often imposed from above,
not developed out of a popular ground wave. This is necessary be-

cause the reactionaries in Islamic society, as often as not, are not at the top of the social ladder but at the bottom. Decisions of courts and of the administration help to formulate human purposes and to give guidance for the future. The very mechanics of democratic procedure may prove educational. A very few rulers in the world still govern according to the divine right of kings; mainly, however, power is legitimated by its assumed delegation by the nation to the monarch, or to representatives of the people.

Traditionally Islam has established authoritarian regimes under the holy law. The Koran does not provide for the divine right of kings, but in fact just such a theory and practice was established.

"Islam legislated the institution of holy war in order to spread its message. Consequently, the religious leader of the Islamic community must concern himself with political power, the means of making war. This is why the prophet originated both a religion and a state, and legislated for both. For if the central characteristic of Islam, the fact that it necessitates the use of political power as a means for propagating itself, is to find practical expression, the leader of the Muslim community must be the head of administration and the leader of the army (*amir al-mu' minîn*), as well as the leader in public prayer (*imâm*). Hence, the supreme office in the Muslim community is the Great Imâmate (*al-imâma al-kubrâ*) which includes all functions and controls all other offices, religious and mundane. This is the religious principle behind the historical fact that the prophet and his true successors in the leadership of the Islamic community aspired to have both religious and political authority, while the leaders of other religious communities, not being in need of using political power for religious purposes, did not have to be concerned with political affairs."[14]

The concentration of power prevails in nearly all Islamic countries rather than the division of powers common in Western governments. In the name of the nation tyrannies are established. Consequently in the fight against oppression, the recipe of the monarchomachs is resorted to with striking frequency: Assassinate the despot! A milder form of limiting the power of the ruler, if not in scope so at least in time, was provided for in the document recording the investiture of Muhammad Ali, which states: "According to time-honored tradition and also according to Islamic law, every nation has the right to install rulers and depose them. Oppressive rulers deviate from the true path of the law, hence the right of nations to depose them."[15]

The issue of unity, of oneness, permeates Arab thought as Hegel had already perceived. The unity of God, the unity of power, the unity of the nation! *Asabiyya,* the "group feeling" or "emotional solidarity complex," *tawhid,* "asserting oneness," *ittihad,* "union," *umma,* "community of believers" or "nation," all these terms are shifted from the religious to the secular political sphere. The circles in which the oneness acts have yet to be drawn. Where oneness does not exist in the present, as in the case of the political shape of the nation, it is projected from a remote past into the future.

Arab nationalism draws more sustenance from religious fountains than Western nationalism has ever done, and this provides it with a particular character. Arab nationalism receives from religion universalist aspirations which carry with them a devaluation of reality and hide the lack of social content. Therefore "the national spirit frequently effervesces and clamors in inverse proportion to its capacity to produce institutions."[16]

Typical of Arab nationalism is its turning back to tradition. It borrows terminology from religion and even its reform movements refer themselves back to their ancestors (*salafiyya*) or consider themselves as originators of a resurrection (*baath*). "Revolution, for many Orientals, means restoration," observes Jacques Berque.[17] But as secularization spreads, nationalism is more and more relied upon as a method to conquer the spiritual and material-technological problems that cannot be avoided in a modern world. Malek Bennabi, himself a member of the *salafiyya* movement, in one of the most brilliant and penetrating analyses written by an Arab struggling with the issues of Western civilization, points out that problems of highest importance are posed to Islamic society but that it does not pose these problems itself.[18] "The incapacity to think and to act . . . the absence of a dialectic link between thought and its concrete end . . . the divorce between thought and action" are weaknesses of Islamic man, who is furthermore hampered by three myths: "We can do nothing, because we are ignorant; we cannot do this because we are poor; we cannot undertake this work, because there is colonialism." These attitudes are, according to Malek Bennabi, the sources of inaction and inadaptability which create a state of *"colonisabilité."* In this state of colonizability conquest by foreigners becomes possible if not inevitable. A static, backward mentality provokes subjection to colonialism.

In this autocriticism, Malek Bennabi finds not enough followers in the Arab world. Nationalists stick to a demonology in which colonialism gets top billing. Westerners tend to see in the emerging nations the proletarians of the modern world. On the basis of alien, imported drugs which reduce disease, prolong life, and increase the birth rate these proletarians, according to widespread Western opinion, produce a "population explosion" and become extremists out of poverty. The underdeveloped nations, however, see their problems not in terms of poverty but in terms of oppression. Being shaken by events and trends which they hardly understand and rarely ever dominate, they personalize their plight and hate colonialists and feudalists, and sometimes Communists and capitalists indiscriminately. The hatred is often strongest in those countries which do not find the strength to refuse foreign aid or alms. Reflected in their nationalistic looking glass, they see not the drab present but the splendor of long-past times, and incur the danger, as Paul Valéry warned, of marching backward into the future.

2. Arab Unity— Islamic Unity

A. Four Elements of Arab Unity

Pan-Arabism constitutes the intellectual main stream of Arab nationalism. But to confer the term "Arab nationalism" exclusively on Pan-Arabism, or on its most violent side-current, Nasserism, would be grossly misleading. Arab nationalism means different things to different groups; it is by no means a simple movement. Pan-Arabism has many facets, and Arab nationalism has assumed three principal forms, which partially or entirely exclude each other. The Arab intelligentsia generally believes in Pan-Arabism, and many politicians pay at least lip service to it. But the movement for unity of all the Arab countries has lost out conspicuously every single time it clashed with local Arab nationalism, a force often widely underestimated. Although in the field of soaring aspirations Pan-Arabism dominates, in the field of reality particularism, local nationalism prevails to the present day. Economic and geographical factors work in a third direction, towards regional integration of the Arab states. Pan-Arab nationalism, local nationalism inside the partly artificial borders of the present Arab states, and regional nationalism grow side by side in competition to each other, and it is too early to predict which of the three will finally get the upper hand.

The belief in the unity of Arab culture and in the unity of all

Arabs is widely shared throughout the Arab countries. Cultural unity, however, does not imply necessarily that political unity can be achieved. The idea of Arab unity is based on the community of language, of law, and of history, all resulting from the unity of religion. There exists no racial unity. The question: Who is an Arab? is answered by the famous sociologist Jacques Berque: "Everybody who feels himself an Arab!" And Abdul Rahman Azzam, former Secretary General of the League of Arab States, provides a more complex definition: "Those who live in Arab lands, speak the Arabic language, live an Arab way of life, and feel proud of being Arab, are Arabs." Abdel Khalek Hassouna, present secretary general of the Arab League, gives still another definition of the term "Arab":

> Today, the term "Arab" generally designates the Arabs as a fixed cultural entity. It designates all the peoples of the Arab world, or in other words the nation which inhabits the lands extending from the Atlantic Ocean to the Arab Gulf. Their assimilation has been accomplished through racial fusion, through the marriage between the Arabs of the Arabian Peninsula and the other regions which are integrated into the Arab world by means of their adopting Arabic as common language and Islam as common religion. One could also say that the Arabs constitute the people that has inherited the Arab traditions, that speaks Arabic and expresses itself in this language. The non-Muslims are not less attached to Arab nationalism than the Muslims.[1]

1. Religion. Islam stands at the beginning of Arab history, or what is experienced as history by the Arabs. Before lies a period of barbarism and ignorance (*ayyam al-jahiliyyah*), pre-history. Islam is not a primitive religion, but the end result of a long development which led to unity, religious unity, and as its outgrowths, linguistic, legal, and historical unity. Islam could never have entered the battlefield successfully against Byzantine and Western Christendom, against Persian Zoroastrism, against South Asian Buddhism, if it had not offered equal or better spiritual values. In the course of only a few generations it expanded as far as China in the East and Spain and France in the West. The people conquered by the sword were quickly converted to Islam, though not as a rule by force, if they were "peoples of the book." Material advantages to be gained by conversion and the overwhelming prestige of the victorious Muslims may have persuaded many to change their religion. Christianity disappeared entirely from North Africa, which had once given to Catholicism many saints and fathers of the church, such as St. Augustine. And Islam progresses steadily in Black Africa to the present day.

An exceptionally solid edifice, Islam resists proselytism even in times of stagnation and decay. Christian missions in Muslim territories have met with little success. Muhammad's introduction of monotheism can be considered as the apotheosis of a unifying process. Language and law derive from the Koran. At al-Azhar University of Cairo, the most important center of education in the Islamic world, the closely connected trinity of sciences—Islamic theology, Islamic law, and Arab language—is taught at the three traditional faculties. Islam, a complex structure, embraces all sectors of daily life, giving simple rules, organizing social relations through religiously sanctioned customs and law, demonstrating an ideal to mankind. A division of religion and politics, of religion and science, or religion and law remains unthinkable as long as Islam is a living force, as long as Islam operates as the single, exclusive motivating force of its creation. "Within the brief span of a mortal life the Arabian Prophet called forth out of unpromising material a nation never before united, in a land that hitherto had been but a geographical expression, and established a religion which in the vast adjacent area superseded Christianity and Judaism and still claims the adherence of some 350,000,000 people—about one-eighth of mankind. . . . With Muhammad, sterile Arabia seems to have been converted, as if by a magic wand, into a breeding-ground of heroes and great men the like of whom in quality and quantity was hard to find."[2]

The Arabs consider Islam as their own special religion, revealed to an Arab, Muhammad, in Arabia in the Arab language.[3] The Koranic revelation, taught and transmitted in Arabic, spread over half the then known world. Like a sandstorm, Arabic buried older languages of highly developed cultures, Aramaic, Coptic, Greek, and Latin. The sword was first to conquer, followed by the Prophet's faith, and only later, in some places centuries later, did spoken Arabic displace other tongues.[4]

Arabic assimilated many foreign elements, but any attempt to eliminate it from a Muslim land meets with enormous resistance. Atatürk's endeavor to extirpate Arabic from the new Turkish national state was followed by a counter movement of surprising strength under the regime of Celal Bayar and Adnan Menderes. The close link between religion and language gives Arabic perhaps the same vigor that Latin acquired through ritual use in the Catholic Church.

A similarly close relationship exists between religion and science. Philology, the science of language, developed in the Arab world out of the necessity to interpret the Koran. And the holy scripture formed classical language as no other work could. This language serves as medium for the written word in all the Arab countries. The dialect of the Prophet became the language of the Arab world and of the holy word in all Islamic regions. As Luther's translation of the Bible created a common language for Germany, so Muhammad's Koran procured a unified language for the Arabs, superseding the different existing dialects. As Hazem Zaki Nuseibeh points out:

> The first and broader process was the dissemination of Islam as a religion in various lands and among different races and cultural backgrounds. The second and narrower process was Arabization, that is, the development—principally in the Middle East and North Africa—of an Arab community of language, of race, and of culture . . . Thus, in a historical setting, Arabism owes to Islam its very existence. A people torn asunder by dissensions and seemingly im-

placable rivalry, a people whose energies were wasted in endless internecine strife and whose mental horizons barely transcended the level of tribal consciousness, in the course of a few years were welded together into a single community, animated by a consciousness of belonging and imbued with a common ideal. . . . That the unifying principle was religion rather than nationality, in that initial phase, is of no practical significance, for as long as Islam was confined to the Peninsula—within which it had attained an unchallenged and monolithic hold—the terms Arab unity and Islamic unity were synonymous and recognized as such.[5]

2. *Language.* Muhammad appears, therefore, as the "creator" of the Arab language used since the seventh century. During the decline of Arab power and Turkish domination of nearly all the Arab lands, Arabic stagnated. The classic language was known only to a minority of the people, the literate, while a variety of dialects developed, especially in the border regions. Even today an Arab from Morocco has difficulty in making himself understood to simple people in Iraq and vice versa. Centrifugal forces revealed themselves in the field of linguistics.

A minority of Muslims in the territories claimed by the Arabs as their own has never accepted Arabic as its language; for instance, the Turkomans, the Armenians and the Indo-European Kurds in the east, and part of the Hamitic Berbers in the west. Some Berber dialects, such as the one in the Soummam Valley used by the late Jean Amrouche, are mixed with Arabic, while others in the remote mountain regions of the Aurès, Kabylia, and the Atlas have preserved a high degree of purity. Arabic in the Maghreb became the written language of the Berbers after the disappearance of Latin and was later superseded by French. The sometime prevalence of Berbers in the Algerian Army of National Liberation (ALN) resulted in the curious fact that a majority of the delegates participating in the peace talks at Evian spoke French as their first, Arabic as their second foreign language, and that French was widely used as the command language in the ALN.

French was at first the principal language of the National Assembly of the Algerian Republic.

Arabic has to overcome the centrifugal forces of the dialects. It is fighting to supplant the non-Arabic vestiges in the Maghreb and on the eastern borders of the Arab lands, and also south of the Sahara, by the language of the Prophet, not only for ritual but also for secular use.[6] Arabic must adjust to the needs of a modern technological civilization with its complicated technical formulas and abstract thoughts. The necessity to reach broader masses for purposes of propaganda and education calls for a simplification of the very structure of the language and even of the typefonts used in the printing of newspapers and books. A vast reform movement is underway, and there remains little doubt that the language of the Koran will be reshaped. Some radical reformers go so far as to wish to substitute Latin letters for the Arabic letters, or to introduce vowels for the "unprintable" accentuation, solutions which run contrary to the religious element in the heritage of the Arabs. All reforms, planned or accomplished, increase the distance between Koranic and modern Arabic. But the reforms are based on the classical language and therefore with progressive mass education tend to eliminate the dialects. By the end of the nineteenth century dialects had nearly destroyed the linguistic unity. The decision of the Arab League, to accept only classic Arabic as the official language of its member states, acts as a strong centripetal force, culturally and, in the long range, politically. Five times a day the Muslim call to prayer resounds from all the minarets in Arabic— it is forever present in Muslim life.

Language for the Arabs is not only a means of communication, but an opiate for the people. "The medium in which the esthetic feelings of the Arabs is mainly (though not exclusively) expressed is that of words and language—the most seductive, it may be, and certainly the most unstable and even dangerous of all the arts. We know something of the effect of the spoken and written word upon ourselves. But upon the Arab mind the impact of artistic

speech is immediate; the words, passing through no filter of logic or
reflection which might weaken or deaden their effect, go straight to
the head," states the Western past master of Islamists, H. A. R.
Gibb.[7] And Edward Atiyah adds: "It is a characteristic of the Arab
mind to be swayed more by words than by ideas, and more by ideas
than by facts. Transcendental principles, especially when put into
resonant speech, seem to the Arabs to have power capable of con-
quering the greatest practical realities."[8] Not that European peoples
are immune to intoxication by words, but words alone rarely assume a value per se (*Wert an sich*). Beautifully turned words put
an Arab into ecstasy; words are taken for the full reality. Western
reality is based on facts, Arab reality may be based on words alone.[9]

3. Law. The law of the Muslim community was originally dis-
tilled out of the Koran. Wilfred Cantwell Smith notes:

> Islamic form was given to almost every aspect of life, what-
> ever its content. And it was an Islamic pattern that gave the society
> cohesion as well as vitality. The center of this unifying force was
> religious law, which regulated within its powerful and precise sweep
> everything from prayer rites to property rights. The law gave unity
> to Islamic society from Cordoba to Multan. It gave unity also to the
> individual Muslim, his entire life activity being organized into a
> meaningful whole by this divine pattern. It gave unity also in time,
> providing the community with continuity, as dynasties rose and fell
> and could be regarded as episodes in the persisting enterprise of
> Islam's endeavor to build on earth the kind of social order that the
> divine imperative prescribes.[10]

According to Islam there is no other source of law than revelation.
Law existed before the Islamic state. As part of the Koran it is of
divine origin, temporal antecedent to the state, which is subordinated to the law. God appears as the one and only lawgiver,
who disclosed the law in His revelations. There remains no room
for a human legislator, be it an individual, or a parliamentary
body. Islamic law knows—after Muhammad—of no Solon, no

Justinian, no Napoleon. Only through *ijma,* the consensus of the believers, can new law be created—a very difficult procedure. "The supreme legislator (*Shāri'*) in Muslim society is God himself. He revealed His laws directly to the Prophet who transmitted them to mankind, first through the Qur'an and secondly, through his customary conduct and practices—the Sunnah. Hence *Shari'a* law is "sacred, infallible and immutable" and the Muslim government is the direct government of God."[11]

Islamic law met with strong resistance even in peoples who otherwise had accepted the new creed. And in some regions of the Arab world it has penetrated only in the last few years. The Bedouins of the Arab desert let themselves be guided by pre-Islamic customs as well as by Islamic laws. Their special rules and customs were guaranteed legal validity until the 1950's by the Arab caliphs, by the Turkish sultans, and by the Western colonial powers. The newly formed national states, Iraq and Syria, abolished the special statutes for the Bedouins, accusing the colonialists of having perpetuated them with the odious aim to divide the Arab world. The Berbers in North Africa, who are Muslims although their religious practice shows heterodox tendencies, were able to retain their customary laws and in practice still keep them. But when the French in Morocco tried to institutionalize the differences between Islamic and Berber customary law by setting up different courts in the so-called Berber Dahir of 1930, a wave of protest shook the Arab, indeed, the Muslim, world. The French were accused of wanting to divide and rule; in fact, they only separated something which had never been united. Had they abolished local customary law they would certainly have been pilloried as destroyers of local culture. In the wake of French rule not only Islamic law spread into the far-away mountain reaches of the Maghreb, but also the Arabic language, so that colonial rule helped, in fact, to spread the unitarian elements in the Arab world.

Non-Muslim communities in the Middle East were permitted throughout history to retain their own particular law of persons under the *millet* (*millah*) system which still prevails in the eastern Arab states and in Israel. Islamic law embraced in theory all sectors of social life, but in practice it was geared to a relatively simple society, and in the more complicated states built after the Arab conquests it could not cover all the aspects of political and economic life. This is discussed by H. A. R. Gibb:

"The science of law," in the words of one of the famous Muslim definitions, "is the knowledge of the rights and duties whereby man is enabled to observe right conduct in this life, and to prepare himself for the world to come. . . ."

The religion of Islam was accepted by a large number of societies, each of which had a long social and legal tradition of its own. In adopting Islam as their religion, the members of those societies also accepted in principle the authority of Islamic law.

The religious leaders of Islam have, in fact, had to engage in a long and arduous struggle to extend the actual jurisdiction of Islamic law among all these peoples. In this struggle they gained a very considerable measure of success, though there are still groups, like the Berbers of Northwest Africa, who are intensely Muslim in feeling, but have even yet preserved their customary law in face of all the efforts of the *ulema* [the learned of Islam].

But here there are some distinctions to be drawn. Although the law embraced, in theory and in the exposition of the jurists, every branch and aspect of social relations, yet there were large areas in the life of the community where it was in practice ignored. The political and administrative institutions, a large part of penal jurisdiction, and most large-scale commerce lay outside its range of effective action, even if their procedures might sometimes be accommodated within its framework by means of legal fictions.[12]

· Large parts of Islamic law became obsolete and were in fact superseded by foreign laws. This process accelerated in the twentieth century to such a degree that in all Arab countries, except Saudi Arabia, Yemen, and the sheikhdoms on the Arab Peninsula, Islamic law has been replaced today by Western laws better adapted for a modern technological civilization based on worldwide trade and cultural interchange. Tunisia has made the longest steps towards total elimination of Islamic law, followed closely by Egypt. Other Arab countries have retained only the Islamic law of persons, while in penal and commercial law the Koranic influence is all but eliminated.

The distinction between public and civil law is unknown in the *Sharia*, which is divine law, God's own will. The Prophet did not set up a durable state organization. The succession was arranged by *ijma*, a sort of tacit plebiscite by the community of believers, who accepted the most deserving and influential of the Prophet's relatives, Abu Bakr, as *imam* (religious leader) and caliph, successor to Muhammad and head of the community. To apply the law, to let every sinner—since transgression was not only a crime but a sin—feel the strength of the law, was the duty of the caliph. His authority derived directly from God. Out of this developed a type of divine right rule.

The derivation of law from God's will reduces human legislation to a minimum. The Muslim order of law seems therefore static and inelastic. The petrification of the legal order reflects itself in the social structure. All believers are equal before God. The original Islamic society shows strong traits of equalitarianism. But equalitarianism should not be taken for democracy. That an Arab can visit his ruler and talk to him more or less as an equal cannot conceal the fact that the ruler's power over other human beings remains practically absolute, limited only by the will of God. It is perhaps no happenstance that in not a single Islamic country has liberal democracy of a Western pattern survived for more than a few years, notwithstanding the constitutions which provided for just such a regime. Turkey might become an exception, because there the struggle between the forces of democracy and of authoritarian rule has, at this time of writing, not yet ended with an irrevocable defeat of the former; but already a general acts as President of the Republic and another former general heads the government. In all other Islamic countries a general, a president, or a king rules

—Hassan II, Bourguiba, Mokhtar ould Daddah, Idriss I, Abdel Nasser, Abboud, Hussein, Ishehab, Saud, Aref, the Shah, the King of Afghanistan, Ayyub, Sukarno, etc.,—and his power is more restricted by the limited material means at his disposal than by a constitution.

Arab society appears as a community of believers in which tribal loyalties easily prevail. The only all-Arab solidarity in history was based on religion and religious law; where religion disappears as a binding force, Arab individualism increases to intolerant solipsism. Ihn Khaldun affirmed that "generally speaking the Arabs are incapable of founding an empire except on a religious basis such as the revelation of a Prophet or a Saint . . . because their fierce character, pride, roughness, and jealousy of one another, especially in political matters, make them the most difficult of peoples to lead, since their wishes concord only rarely. . . . Every Arab regards himself as worthy to rule, and it is rare to find one of them submitting willingly to another, be it his father, or his brother, or the head of his clan, but only grudgingly."[13]

The intolerance and jealousy of Arabs toward each other, described by Ibn Khaldun, seems certainly one of the most striking features of social and political relations in the Arab world. Declamations of friendship are immediately followed by vicious denunciations, but, on the other hand, the Arab who has tried to sink a dagger in another Arab's back can be hailed the next day as a brother. "Wherever they went, the Arabs carried with them their intense, jealously guarded individualism and their aversion to all authority save that of their own tribal leaders, to whom they were bound by ties of kinship."[14]

Gamal Abdel Nasser expresses his disgust about Arab egotism, the extent of which he realized with a shock after the revolution of July 23, 1952: "Had I been asked then what I required most, my instant answer would have been, 'To hear but one Egyptian uttering one word of justice about another, to see but one Egyptian not devoting his time to criticizing wilfully the ideas of another, to feel that there was but one Egyptian ready to open his heart to forgiveness, indulgence, and love for his brother Egyptians.' Personal and persistent selfishness was the rule of the day. The word 'I' was on every tongue. It was the magic solution of every difficulty and the effective cure for every malady. I often met men, referred to in the press as 'great men,' of various tendencies and colors, from whom I sought the solution of a difficult problem. I could hear nothing from them save the word 'I'. . . ."[15]

The role of law as unifying factor can hardly be overestimated. H. A. R. Gibb affirms:

> Islamic law was the most far-reaching and effective agent in molding the social order and the community life of the Muslim peoples. By its very comprehensiveness it exerted a steady pressure upon all private and social activities, setting a standard to which they conformed more and more closely as time went on, in spite of the resistance of ancient habits and time-honored customs, especially amongst the more independent nomadic and mountain tribes. Moreover, Islamic law gave practical expression to the characteristic Muslim quest for unity. In all essentials it was uniform, although the various schools differed in points of detail. To its operation was due the striking convergence of social ideals and ways of life throughout the medieval Muslim world. It went far deeper than Roman law; by reason of its religious bases and its theocratic sanctions it was the spiritual regulator, the conscience of the Muslim community in all its parts and activities.[16]

Islamic law did not give way to foreign laws without a struggle. Even after the breakup of the Arab Caliphate, the united Arab empire, Muslims continued to accept the *Sharia*. But a change of character was inevitable. G. E. von Grunebaum points out:

> The gradual drifting away of canon law from operational effectiveness, its character as a moral code, a *Pflichtenlehre* (rather than a regulatory code of community relations), called forth by and calling forth the growing encroachment of local custom and governmental decree as directives in most areas of practical living, again

fortified the catholicity of the Muslim institution. It did so in two complimentary ways. On the one hand, it facilitated the integration into the community of as yet alien communities by allowing them to carry over into their existence as Muslims much of their traditional way of life; on the other hand, it provided the community with a norm that was all the more readily acceptable because to a large extent there was no insistence on full compliance. So the canon law became one of the strongest cementing factors among disparate communities which continued much of their customary law.[17]

The gradual disappearance of Muslim law in the modern world eliminates one of the main features of Arab unity.

4. History. How could Arab history be conceived without Islam? Arab history begins with Muhammad's biography; what lies before is only pre-history, and to the Arabs only pre-history's highly developed poetry seems very relevant. "Historical consciousness was brought to the Arabs first by the Koran with its all-embracing picture of the religious history of mankind, punctuated by the sending of a series of prophets."[18] Genealogy for a long time took the place of history in the Arab world. Interminable "family trees" proved one's descent from high-born personalities or prestigious tribes. The conflict between Qahtan and Adnan, the descendents of South Arabian and North Arabian tribes, tracing their ancestry as far back as Abraham's sons, remains a relevant factor of social and political life and strife in Jordan and even in Westernized Lebanon. But "both Qahtanities and Adnanities united against non-Arabs, whom they called *ajam* (dumb), boasting of the superiority of their own race and language."[19]

Scientists "proved" their theories by reference to long lines of authorities. Tradition in both instances was built on personal relationship. The traditions held man on the indestructible umbilical cord of ancestral authority, hampering a free development, intellectually and socially. Religion alone allowed for a transition from the limited tribe-centered thinking into universal spheres.

Islam formed the Arab mentality and culture and was in turn influenced by them. Even non-Muslim Arabs and non-Arab Muslims are deeply motivated by the same ethnic-religious features as the Muslim Arabs. The symbiosis of Arabism and Islam could not be closer. The only unified Arab empires were formed on the basis of Islamic solidarity. Hazem Zaki Nuseibeh states:

> In the circumstances of its rise, therefore, Islam's great gift to the Arabs was the creation of a community and the establishment of a state. . . . To Islam is due the birth of a nation, the birth of a state, the birth of a national history, and the birth of a civilization. The reasons have been discussed at some length: (1) the emergence of a community to which the innate instinct of patriotism could be applied in place of the narrow-gauged loyalty to locality and tribe; (2) the emergence of a political organization around which traditions of habitual loyalty could gather, thus supplanting the conditions of near anarchy existing hitherto; (3) the launching of the Arab people on a career of national glory which, in a few years, put them on the political map of the world; and (4) the emergence of a civilization which they could cherish and to which they could look for inspiration and guidance.[20]

History for the Arab is largely looking backward to the glorious time of the Prophet and the Umayyad and Abbassid empires, the flowering of poetry and science, the refined casuistry of law. Looking back, he sees unity everywhere, especially if he disregards the dissensions after the eighth century and the decay of the Arab Empire. In the period of greatest decadence unity was reestablished by the Turks. The beginning of Turkish rule coincided with the opening of the sea route from the European Atlantic coast —Portugal—to India and Southeast Asia, the Spice Islands, and even China, and with the destruction of Arab sea power and trade in the Indian Ocean by the Portuguese. As a result the Middle East lost its function as main trade route between Europe and Asia, until the opening of the Suez Canal and, more recently, the air routes over the land bridge between three continents. Turkish domination over most of the Arab lands from 1516-17 to 1918 left the illusion of continued unity, but, in fact, the crumbling away had already started with the French occupation of Algiers in 1830. Turkish administration was hardly conducive to high cultural development in the Arab regions, but since it was at least Islamic rule it was not felt as a completely alien reign. But "the political fragmentation which followed the breakup of the Ottoman Empire after World War I, and the varied foreign influences which accompanied that breakup, created a multitude of parochial interests, attitudes, loyalties, and prejudices, which, according to what seems to be the 'iron law of oligarchy,' tend to be self-perpetuating."[21] One might add that under the Ottoman Empire the Arabs involuntarily enjoyed a greater degree of unity than ever in the last thousand years. Joseph F. Schacht says:

> One ancient Arab idea . . . became the central concept of Islamic religious law and theology, and asserted itself as the second most important single contribution of the Arabs to the civilization which arose in the Islamic empire. I mean the idea of tradition, precedent, or, in Arabic, *sunna*. The Arabs were, and are, bound by tradition and precedent, they were, and are, dominated by the past.[22]

Few attempts have been made by Arab historians to set the Arab past in world-wide perspective. It is mythologized or warped for political purposes. Abdul Rahman Azzam uses alleged or real Arab infiltrations for "several thousand years" before Muhammad into the Euphrates and Nile valleys, to assert the unity of the Arab world and to counteract local nationalism justified by the existence of pre-Arab culture in Egypt and in Iraq.[23] Reading Arab political writers—last but not least, Gamal Abdel Nasser—one has to remind oneself time and again that history is not exclusively a continuous set of personal intrigues and conspiracies. The personalization of history clouds the real issues and hides the battle of ideas going on everywhere in the world.

The struggle between tradition and innovation continues in

Arab society. In a spiritual sense, tradition still holds its own; at least Islam has not seen any reformation of the type Christianity underwent in the sixteenth century. Whoever wants to dissent now breaks away completely from the fetters of Islam and seeks a new spiritual stance in the secular religions of nationalism and communism.

The big Islamic reform movement initiated by Jamal ed-Din al-Afghani and Muhammad Abduh, lies in the past—Afghani died in 1897, Abduh in 1905. Their "enlightened puritanism" did not want to westernize Islamic society but to defend it with the weapons of modern thinking against Western-Christian influences. Significantly, the movement chose the name *salafiyya,* from *salaf* (ancestor), indicating that it wanted to go back to the pure doctrine of the ancestors. "The *salafiyya* gave impulses for a number of Islamic-integralist mass movements, for instance the Muslim Brotherhood in Egypt, which is, however, far removed from the high standards of Muhammad Abduh. The historic-political significance of the *salafiyya* lies in the fact that it has aroused a new intellectual-religious feeling of community in the framework of Sunnite orthodoxy. Modern Arabism found in this soil one of its roots, even if it has been a long time since it was mainly based on religion."[24]

Subtle interpretation of Koranic law took the place of theological criticism. "The Islamic counterpart to the Christian theologian has been the legist: the Muslim's supreme duty has been less to know the truth than to do the right."[25] The right is found in tradition. "In essence Islamic history, therefore, is the fulfilment, under divine guidance, of the purpose of human history . . . . The fundamental spiritual crisis of Islam in the twentieth century stems from an awareness that something is awry between the religion which God has appointed and the historical development of the world which He controls."[26] The obvious question arises: Where lies the way out of this spiritual dilemma?

B. The Bonds of Islam

1. Universalism. Muhammad addressed himself in the Arabic language to Arabs in an Arab land. But his message was universal. It was soon carried by conquerors and missionaries as far east as China and south into Black Africa. The community of Arab believers became a community of Muslims, the *umma al-arabiyyah* developed into the *umma al-islamiyyah*. But in modern times the term *umma* has been used to designate the nation, a social or political unit which adds up to more than its component parts. A socio-religious term was used for a political concept. Other terms for "people," like *qawm* or *shaab* or *millah* (*milla*) or maybe even *watan* (fatherland), could have been extensively interpreted and given the sense of nation. The Turks, in a similar terminology, use the word *millet* for nation, the equivalent of *millah*. Ziya Gökalp, the foremost promoter of a Turkish nationalist ideology, discusses this problem:

> When we look at social realities, we cannot fail to see that an Islamic *ümmet,* an Ottoman state (*devlet*), a Turkish or an Arab nation (*millet*) do exist. However, if this statement corresponds to any reality, the term "ümmet" must denote the totality of those people who profess the same religion, the "state" all those who are administered under the same government, and the "nation" all those who speak the same language. The statement will be valid and will correspond to reality only if the above definitions are accepted. It seems, then, that those who do not accept this statement deny it, not because its meaning does not correspond to reality, but because they do not believe that these words are suitable for denoting the respective meanings. The Islamists say that the word "nation" (*millet,* Arabic *milla*) denotes what we cover by the word "ümmet." The term "milla," they say, means "sect" in Arabic... The term "ümmet" or religious community corresponds to the term "église" (church), and therefore we can use it in this sense because we already use such

47

expressions as "Muhammedan ümmet," "Christian ümmet," "Mosaic ümmet," as well as the ümmet of Islam, ümmet of Ijabah (the people who obey a prophet's call), of Davah (the people invited by a prophet), etc.[27]

Language, law, and history for the Arabs are founded on religion. Religion claims universal validity, absolute validity in space and time, since it transmits the one and only, the eternal truth. Its claim to validity is universal. This universalism the Arabs transpose into modern politics, where it appears as incongruous as would the Christian universalism of the Middle Ages if transferred to the twentieth century. The choice of the word "umma" for "nation" is a religious-universal term for a basically political-particularistic concept and shows clearly the different spiritual context in which Arab and European nationalism develop.

The Arab *umma* of the early Middle Ages could claim "universal" power in the same way that Christendom felt itself universal. The barriers between the Arab-Muslim and the European Christian world were high and sharp. What lay outside these barriers was another world, another galaxy; it was barbarian domain. Christendom in the west, the Arab Empire in the south and east formed closed self-sufficient circles outside which no value was conceded, somewhat similar on a larger scale to the famous Hungarian chauvinist saying: *Extra Hungarian non est vita.* . . .

"Universal" in the Middle Ages meant at one and the same time, both more and less than "global." Neither Islam nor Christianity had renounced their universal appeal in theory; in practice, however, closed, restricted communities were formed. Whoever remained outside the community of Christian believers was thought of as condemned to eternal perdition because he had never heard of Jesus Christ. In this limited sense, an element of universalism has crept into Pan-Arab nationalism: all the Arabs, all the members of the *umma al-arabiyyah* do belong to the Arab nation and must adhere to its desired political form. Furthermore, all the territories once conquered by Islam must revert to the Islamic realm even if they have been for centuries in non-Muslim hands.

Islam as a religion aspires to universalism. Nationalism based on Islam contains a strong admixture of universalism in the medieval sense, when the Arab world was indeed a world in itself, fighting the Christian world on the shores of the Mediterranean and flowing into the pagan (non-monotheistic) regions of Africa and Asia. The Arab "world" today is only a little province of the globe, whose inhabitants are brought steadily nearer to each other— sometimes kicking and screaming—by modern means of communication.

"Nationalism for Muslims is everywhere a Muslim nationalism."[28] The dichotomy between the different value systems of Islam and of nationalism seems obvious; however, it has never been overcome in political practice. "The attitude of an Arab nationalist is that the entire legacy of Islam, insofar as it was expressed in Arabic and arose in an Arab milieu, is his heritage."[29] This refers especially to the Pan-Arab nationalists of yesterday and today.

2. Religious and Secular Nationalism. Pan-Arab nationalism is inconceivable without its obvious religious foundations, just as Jewish nationalism, which has found its fulfilment in the creation of an independent Israel, cannot be imagined without the cement of religion. Bear in mind, however, that religion in the Arab world has ceased to be the main motivating force. Arab nationalism in all its forms is not a movement aimed at re-establishing religious unity and predominance. But is it an entirely secular movement, as many nationalists and foreign observers see it? Georges Hanna exclaims: "Arabism is not Islam, and Islam is not Arabism."[30] Marouf al-Dawalibi, Syrian Prime Minister in early 1962, asserts: "During the Jahiliyyah, the Arabs were Arabs without having been Muslims . . . it is not possible to consider religion in general as one of the basic elements of Arab nationalism."[31] Philip K. Hitti declares Arab nationalism a Western import:

> Arab nationalism, like other nationalisms, was a modern Western import, stemming mainly from French political thought . . . Islam recognizes no physical, no geographical boundaries—only religious ones—, is universal in its outlook, international and supernational; it emphasizes spiritual rather than economic values. Nationalism of the latter-day brand demands loyalty that transcends and if necessary suppresses all other loyalties, not excepting the religious. It recognizes no sectarian classification and can thrive only in a secular society. In its extreme manifestation it becomes itself a religion. That is why as a conscious purposeful movement it made no headway in Arab lands until the first World War. It did not seep down and move the masses until the sufferings of the war were felt and the Woodrow Wilson doctrine of self-determination was expounded. The modern term for it, *qawmiyah,* was not coined till the twentieth century.[32]

Wilfred Cantwell Smith on the other hand cautions that "some writers have been too hasty in assuming or concluding that a Western-type nationalism in this positive sense could be or has been adopted fairly easily or effectively into the Islamic world. . . . It was the Islamic impetus that carried the Arabs from their obscure home into historic greatness, in conquest and creativity. Islam gave the Arabs earthly greatness; and vice versa, it was the Arabs who gave Islam its earthly success . . . . The synthesis is close: an identification, at times unconscious, of Islam and Arabism. On the one hand, an Arab need not be pious or spiritually concerned in order to be proud of Islam's historic achievements. Indeed, he need not even be a Muslim; Christian Arabs have taken a share in that pride."[33] In fact Christians have played an enormous role in the initial stages of the birth of Arab nationalism, and some Christians, like Michel Aflaq, are still leaders of a nationalist movement.

"The idea of Arab nationalism had begun among Christian intellectuals before it did among Muslims. The Christians had been more strongly exposed to Western cultural influences, and they had read Arab history through the lenses of modern Western scholarship,"[34] asserts Hazem Zaki Nuseibeh. He goes on to state: "Diffidence and ambiguity have kept important sections of the Christian Arabs lukewarm and suspicious, for they fear, with some justification, that Arab nationalism without a more forthright reorientation along secular lines may be no more than a façade for an Islamic policy, to which they naturally could not subscribe."[35]

Nuseibeh believes that "George Antonius' account of the nationalist movement shows unmistakably the preponderant role of the Christian Arabs, particularly in the early phase. At least half the works on Arab nationalism cited in the present book [*The Ideas of Arab Nationalism*] are by Christian Arabs."[36]

Many Arab writers consider Islam as a constituent element of Arab nationalism. Leaving aside the protagonists of Pan-Islamism, it may be pointed out that Gamal Abdel Nasser tries to find a religious basis even for his Arab socialism. Muhammad Abdallah al-Arabi, who presents the ideology of Abdel Nasser, asserts that the economic and political system of Arab nationalism is Islamic as opposed to secular.[37] A French economist, Jacques Austruy, feels that "Arab nationalism is a means to translate into modern terms the solidarity of the *umma* and the revolt of Islam against foreign occupation."[38]

The question of the relationship between Islam and Arabism has caused many discussions between Western Islamists. An Iraqi student sums up the divergences of opinion in the following way:

> Blachère divides scholars into two camps when discussing a similar question to the one treated now. According to him, Nöldeke, Arnold, and Goldziher believe in the universal message of the Qur'an, while Grimme, Snouck-Hurgronje, Lammens, and Buhl believe that the Qur'an is meant for the Arabs only. . . . One might

say that the Qur'an preaches universal brotherhood and love in a conditioned sense, that is, the universality does not embrace the whole of mankind unless all men believe in the message of the Qur'an. . . . That some Qur'anic arguments side with Arabism in one way or another there seems to be no doubt. But these arguments are overwhelmed by arguments which base the notions of brotherhood and love on an *ummah* of men whose essential relationship with each other is a common belief in an ideology. . . . The logic of the Qur'an seems to reconcile the trend of Arabism with that of the *ummah* rather than to consider them as conflicting with one another. A critic might observe in this reconciliation some sort of onesidedness for two reasons:

Firstly, a non-Arab in accepting the message of Qur'an can only receive it in the best way by learning Arabic and swallowing Arabism. In other words, as the Qur'an is in Arabic and it is the last and most authoritative word of God, then the weight of Arabism in the *ummah* is surely not mean.

Secondly, other prophets sent by God to other *ummahs*, together with their followers, are in a general sense Moslems—i.e. submissive to God. Hence, proper Moslems are instructed to love and to treat kindly and fairly other communities of similar ideologies to that of the Qur'an. But there again it is the Qur'an which decides— it is the Qur'an which shows the common roots and the differences.[39]

How can these contradictory statements and observations about Arab nationalism be explained? Is nationalism a secular movement or are its religious foundations only incidentals, with no influence on its modern development? Remember that nationalism means different things to different men. Nationalism can appear as a unifying force—as it did in Germany and Italy—but Pan-Germanism never did succeed completely, and even Italy never convinced all the Italian-speaking peoples that they should be united under one regime. Nationalism may act as a divisive force —as in the Balkans—where on the ruins of the supra-national empires of the Habsburgs and the Osmanlis unrest and strife prevailed, until under Soviet rule peace ensued—the peace of the graveyard.

Not a few early nationalists appealed to heaven to prove the validity of their newly expounded creed. Herder, Fichte, Mazzini, and John Quincy Adams, different as they were, all believed that God created nations according to his will. Greek nationalism—as manifested lately in Cyprus—was not only justified by the unity of creed and rite but also developed in closest co-operation with the Orthodox church and its hierarchy. On the other hand, most European nationalists ended up in a *Kulturkampf,* a fight of the secular powers against the Catholic church, with the result a division of church and state.

No new and lasting social order can be created until a world view (Weltanschauung) is established. Nationalism tries hard to evolve or institute a new world view, but before it has done so—and often after seeing its inability to achieve this aim—it very often borrows from earlier ideologies or philosophies. Michel Aflaq proclaims: "Arab nationalism is not theoretical but gives rise to theories; it is not the product of thought but nourishes it." Aflaq, the only creator of an ideology in the Arab world, obviously refers to the emotional basis of nationalism which precedes the theoretical.

Pan-Arabism appears as a composite of different heterogeneous movements. At times it emerges linked to Pan-Islamism, which obviously pursues different goals, then again it proclaims itself as wholly secularized, then again it uses Islam as an instrument —consciously or inconsciously—for nationalist aims. That Islam provides the foundation and cement of what exists of Arab unity, i.e., language, etc., does not mean that Pan-Arab nationalism must lead to Pan-Islamism or to a theocratic state.

3. Mutations of Nationalism. Arab nationalism in the two generations since its inception has undergone changes and mutations. It started out closely linked to Pan-Islamism, and it is not by sheer concidence that Jamal ed-Din al-Afghani and Muhammad Abduh, Pan-Islamists and religious-political reformers, are always mentioned in connection with the birth of Arab nationalism. Strictly political nationalism lifted its head in the last years of Turkish rule when the Young Turks attempted to "ottomanize" the empire. This early nationalism clearly had particularistic overtones; it was secular and did not transgress a limited circle. In many instances Christians appeared as its leaders, and few thought of unifying all the Arab lands from the Atlantic to the Indian Ocean.

The disappearance of the Ottoman Empire and the domination of the Arab lands by non-Islamic European powers gave rise to new currents of nationalism, which before 1914 had caused only a few ripples on the surface of the Middle East and North Africa. Nationalism branched out in three different directions and it is important to distinguish the various divisions. In the newly created non-sovereign and sovereign Arab states local nationalism increased between the world wars, nationalism of a European type, secular and with a limited scope of independence. Regional integration attracted a few leaders, but it was pursued mainly for dynastic reasons by the Hashemites, first in Mecca, later in Amman and Baghdad. Pan-Arab nationalism found numerous adherents among the intelligentsia, but politically it lacked organizers to galvanize the massses into action and to give them a concrete aim, the unification of all the Arab countries. Only after World War II did Pan-Arabism as a political movement raise its head, and while its influence spread, it had to reach back to Islam, the one unifying force in Arab history, the one which had more than anything else determined Arab history. To counteract the divisive forces of secular nationalism, Pan-Arabism mobilized the unifying forces of Islam. The Christian masses in the Middle East, more sensitive to traditional pressures than their Europeanized intellectual leaders, feel strongly the resurgence of Islamic forces incorporated in Pan-Arabism and they resist it if necessary—for instance in Lebanon and Jordan—with all their strength.

Arnold Toynbee points out the difficulty of co-ordinating the forces of religion and of nationalism: "It is not easy to make a national religion of Christianity or Islam. The appeal of these two missionary religions is not local but universal. They address themselves to each individual. Both their universalism and their individualism are genuine, and this puts them at loggerheads with nationalism, since nationalism's idol is some particular fraction of the human race."[40]

Nationalism, however, is not logical. And Arab nationalism needs regress to the unifying forces set in motion by Muhammad to mobilize the masses and overcome the individualism of the Arabs. Toynbee believes that "for the time, at any rate, nationalism has supplanted the nominal religions in fact, though not avowedly. Only communism has been able to stand up to nationalism, and this only in non-Communist countries." In some instances nationalism is riding piggyback on old religions before supplanting them altogether. Toynbee himself stresses the close relationship between Islam and politics: "Indeed, Islam became a successful religion only after it had become a successful state—and, what is more, it owed its eventual triumph as a religion to its previous political success. . . . . Ever since Mohammed's withdrawal from Mecca to Medina, Islam has been implicated in politics. Perhaps the present-day invasion of the Islamic world by Western nationalism may at last give Islam an opportunity to shake off the unfortunate incubus of its political past."[41] Religion in Africa, according to Toynbee, has passed through a succession of phases in a single century: "From magic and nature-worship to Islam and Christianity; from these to nationalism; and, through nationalism, back toward the pre-Islamic and pre-Christian dispensation."[42]

The moment Arab nationalism turns back to its pre-Islamic past, as it does in the case of certain writers and politicians, it reverts to particularism. The pre-Islamic past of Iraq is not Arab, but Sumerian, Babylonian, and Assyrian; the pre-Islamic past of Lebanon is Phoenician; of Palestine it is Hebrew; of Egypt it is Pharaonic; and of the Maghreb it is Berber—not to mention the "Western" domination by Greeks and Romans. Some nationalists, like Abdul Rahman Azzam, want to bridge the gap by asserting that Semitic peoples had formed, or at least influenced, the ancient empires.[43] But not all Semites are Arabs. In North Africa the Semitic Phoenicians settled only the fringes of the Berber dominions of the interior. The ambivalence of Maghrebian nationalism becomes clear in the search for "ancestors" to modern attitudes. The official newspaper of the Algerian National Liberation Front, *El Moudjahid*, proclaims: "The Algerian nation was formed starting with the upheaval caused thirteen centuries ago in North Africa by the arrival of the Arabs and the Islamization of the Maghrebian peoples."[44] But in a later edition *El Moudjahid* goes farther back in history and writes: "It was an Algerian, Massinissa, who for the first time in the history of mankind stated the principle of nationalism. . . . Our national heroes: Jugurtha, Tacfarinas, etc. . . ."[45]

In these two statements the different historical roots of modern nationalism are clearly evidenced. If the Algerians reach back to their Berber past, the fighters against Roman rule, then their feeling of solidarity with the Arab countries is not strengthened. On the other hand, it was the religious bond which distinguished the Muslim fighters for an independent Algeria from the Christian and Jewish protagonists of an *Algérie française*. And this basic cleavage remains, even though more Muslims were enrolled in the French security forces than fought with the Army of National Liberation. The Algerian Muslims have not given way to any religious fanaticism but adhere to the principles of a secular state. An Algerian nation as such never existed, as Ferhat Abbas himself, later Prime Minister of the rebel Provisional Government of the Algerian Republic, once acknowledged; the people were formed into a nation only during their fight against the French. Their cohesion is founded on the community of their religious background and their opposition to the French. While many Berbers cannot be distinguished physically from Southern Europeans, they were segregated from their non-Muslim neighbors by the barriers of religion, which gave them separate laws and customs and made them distinguishable from non-Muslims of North African birth.

Ziya Gökalp, the Turkish nationalist, believes that language and religion are constituent elements of national consciousness (quoting a Turkish proverb: "The one whose language is my language, and whose faith is my faith, is of me"); he points out an important function of religion in the formation of the cultural unity of nations:

> As language plays a part in deciding religious affiliation, so religion plays a part in determining membership in a nationality. The Protestant French became Germanized when they were expelled from France and settled in Germany. The Turkish aristocracy of the old Bulgars became Slavicized following their conversion to Christianity. And today, the non-Turkish Muslims migrating to Turkey in a scattered way are becoming Turkified because of their religious affiliation. We may conclude, therefore, that there is a close relationship between linguistic and religious association.[46]

While Arab-Turkish relations were described by many Western writers in terms of the Arab resistance against Young Turkish centralization in 1908 and in terms of the romanticized "revolt in the desert," lately it has been pointed out by Zeine N. Zeine that relatively little Arab opposition to Turkish rule was felt in the four centuries since Sultan Selim conquered the greater part of the Arab world: "The Arabs as Muslims were proud of Turkish power and prestige. The Ottoman Empire was their Empire as much as it was the Turks' . . . But it must be remembered that during the greatest part of Turkish rule the Arabs did not consider the Turkish rule as a 'foreign' rule. . . . The vast majority of the Arabs did not consider the Turks as 'foreigners'—except when the Turkish leaders themselves, after 1908, ceased to be considered in the Arab eyes as good Muslims and defenders of Islam and as brothers in the Faith."[47]

In the case of Turkish-Arab relations, nationalism—first Turkish, later Arab nationalism—split the Muslim peoples apart to such a degree that many modern Turks feel hardly any connection any more with the Arabs. The Arabs themselves were split apart by the borders drawn by or with the connivance of Western powers and divided by the ensuing local loyalties. This was all the more easy because the old social structures of the Arab community had not withstood the onslaught of Western civilization and had been destroyed. Turkish nationalism and Turkish secularization broke down the bridges which had linked Turks and Arabs since Turkish slaves and mercenaries had first been brought into the decaying Abbassid Empire. There they helped administer and defend the Empire, later creating their own diadochal principalities on the ruins of the shattered Arab domains and finally re-creating their own empire under the Osmanli sultan-caliphs. The disappearance of the Ottoman Empire after 1918 threw the Arabs back to the disunion of pre-Ottoman times.

4. Pan-Islamism. Islam is doubtlessly the main source of Arab unity. But to what degree is it still active as a political force? Islamic forces operate politically in two different directions: they work for Pan-Islamic unity or they act to re-establish Koranic law and customs in the different Muslim states. Agitating for Pan-Islamic unity they clash with the different brands of Arab nationalism whose "universe" at the most is restricted to the Arab "world." Pan-Islamism seems, for all practical political purposes, a force of the past which can never be revived. Its remainders, however, can be used for other political purposes. The last Ottoman sultans' appeal to Pan-Islamic feelings failed to mobilize any notable sympathies for Abdul Hamid, and they also failed to gain support for Turkey in World War I. Sherif Hussain's later attempt to give new life to the caliphate abolished by the Turks met with complete failure. Nevertheless, at least three different organizations are today at work in Arab countries, trying to keep alive the Pan-Islamic ideals and using them at the same time for specific political purposes.

One of these organizations is the Islamic Congress in Cairo, created by Gamal Abdel Nasser in collaboration with the heads of state of Pakistan and Saudi-Arabia. Anwar as-Sadat, right hand man of the Egyptian President, took over the direction with the title of Secretary General. The executive council should have been formed by the heads of state of the Islamic peoples, but nothing came of this project. Pakistan did not even pay its dues, and Saudi Arabia stopped its payments after the first year or so. What remains is strictly an Egyptian rump organization which uses religion for its political purposes, especially in its propaganda in Black Africa, where Islam is still advancing. A "Voice of Islam" has joined the "Voice of the Arabs" and the "Voice of Palestine" and other instruments of the Cairo propaganda. Teachers and experts are sent out all over the Islamic world and carry the word of Gamal Abdel Nasser as far as Malaya and Indonesia and south into equatorial Africa. Every Muslim, wherever he lives, is considered *ipso jure* a member of the Islamic Congress. Abdel Nasser strives for, so he says in his *Philosophy of the Revolution*, "a co-operation that does not deprive them of their loyalty to their countries but which guarantees for them and their brethren a limitless power."[48]

Abdel Nasser is mobilizing the forces of Islam more today than in the first years of his rule. His interest in Muslim Africa grows, and in that part of the world Islam is progressing at a fairly fast rate. Whoever wants to acquire status, to move up in the world, renounces paganism and converts himself to monotheism. And Islam seems to the pagan more easily accessible than Christianity. Abdel Nasser's belief in Islam appears genuine. He personally follows the rituals of his religion—not just for public display—and he takes part in the community prayer on Friday. "Can we ignore that there is a Muslim world with which we are tied by bonds which are not only forged by religious faith but also tightened by the facts of history?" exclaims Abdel Nasser.[49] The Islamic world is named by the *rais* (leader) as the third circle "which should be the theater of our activity and in which we try to move as much as we can." He proclaims his "faith in the positive efficacy which can be the outcome of further strengthening the Islamic bonds with all other Muslims."[50] And he continues with a grandiose vision: "When my mind travels to the eighty million Muslims in Indonesia, the fifty million in China, and the several other million in Malaya, Siam, and Burma, and the hundred million in Pakistan, the hundred million or more in the Middle East, and the forty million in Russia, as well as the other millions in the distant parts of the world, when I visualize these millions united in one faith, I have a great consciousness of the tremendous potentialities that co-operation amongst them all can achieve."[51]

Abdel Nasser exploits Pan-Islamism. When newspapers announced that Iran would grant Israel diplomatic recognition, Cairo appealed to all the Muslims to oppose the Shah's move. Since Iran is by no means an Arab country, the Egyptian agitation against Israel unfolded on the basis of Muslim—not Arab—solidarity.

The Cairo government at one time planned to send out "religious attachés" to foreign capitals. To spread the faith, an Islamic World Center was founded in Cairo, and students from all the world are invited to study at al-Azhar University. While the Egyptian Muslim influence exerted in South and East Asia is very limited, and even in the Middle East it meets decided opposition, in the "Casablanca" states—the United Arab Republic, Morocco, Ghana, Guinea, Mali, and Algeria—and in other parts of Africa it is increasing.

Abdel Nasser even tries to justify his "Arab socialism" by the Koran and by the early Muslim practices. Socialism, however, appears as the secular antithesis of Islam. Which of the different elements, nationalism, socialism, or Islam, in Abdel Nasser's ideology will eventually prevail remains to be seen. Secularism seems irreversible, but Zeine N. Zeine, an acute observer of the Middle Eastern scene, suggests that the forces of Islam are still stronger than those of secular nationalism:

> The true birth of Arab nationalism took place with the rise of Islam. The Arab nation was, thus, a nation originally born of Islam. This 'religious nationalism' remains an indelible part of the hearts and minds of the Arabs . . . The force of Islam is still much greater than the force of politico-secular nationalism.[52]

One of the ironies of modern Middle Eastern politics is that the two other international Islamic organizations are directed against Abdel Nasser. The Islamic Conference, with seat in Jerusalem, acts in competition with the Islamic Congress in Cairo. Religious and political organizations of conservative tendencies are members of the Islamic Conference. King Hussein of Jordan and President Habib Bourguiba of Tunisia hold a benevolent hand over the Conference. Its activity extends as far west as Morocco and deep into Black Africa. Bourguiba's support is especially noteworthy because the Tunisian leader has pushed secularization in his country farther than has any other Arab chief of state.

The third effort to mobilize the traditionalist forces of Islam for political purposes was launched in Mecca in May, 1962,[53] when under King Saud's leadership, two hundred leading Muslims who had participated in the pilgrimage to Mecca formed a "League of the Islamic World" with a twenty-one man executive council to carry out its program. Muhammad Surur Sabban, a former minister in Saudi Arabia, was named Secretary General of the new organization. Its proclaimed objective was to form an Islamic Commonwealth. The League polemized in a series of resolutions against the alleged oppression of Muslims in India and Ethiopia, against atomic tests in Africa, against prostitution, alcohol, gambling, and usury. But its main battle front was directed against socialism— Marxian or Nasserian—and communism.

5. Islamic Parties. In different Arab countries organizations have emerged which proclaim the return to Islamic law and the revival of Islamic beliefs as the principal aim of their political activity. The most famous of these groups is doubtless the Muslim Brotherhood.[54] The founder, Hassan al-Banna, explains that a spiritual awakening is the principal objective of his movement, an awakening based on the original teachings of Islam by the *salafiyya*. The Muslim Brotherhood would fight for independence based on Islam and not on Western theories which, Hassan al-Banna asserts, have invaded the Middle East with their education, capitalism, politics, and moral decadence. Hassan al-Banna fought with word and dagger against the alleged Westernizers in Egypt, and he himself fell victim to a counterplot. His successors for a while maintained close contacts with the Free Officers of Muhammad Nagib and Gamal Abdel Nasser, but after an assassination attempt against the latter by a member of the Muslim Brotherhood at Alexandria on October 26, 1954, the movement was ruthlessly suppressed in Egypt and, after the *Anschluss* of Syria, also in that country. It lifted its head for a while after the break between Syria and Egypt. The relatively weak affiliated organization in Jordan was banned, along with all other political groups, by King Hussein after the disturbances in the spring of 1957.

In the fight for an independent Algeria, the Association of the Ulemas, although not a political party, played an important political role. After the outbreak of a full-scale war of liberation on November 1, 1954, the Association of Ulemas joined the National Liberation Front. One of the leading members of the Association, Tewfik al-Madani, was variously a member of the Provisional Government of the Algerian Republic and its representative in Cairo. Later, he became minister for religious foundations (*habous*) in the government of Ben Bella.

Sheikh Takieddin al-Nabhani's Liberation (Tahrir) party suffers the misfortune of being banned in Jordan, where its Palestinian leader first organized it, in Lebanon, where he lives, and in Syria. The fact that Nabhani and many of his followers have been arrested repeatedly in Lebanon for disturbance of the religious peace, reflects the weakness of the Liberation party, which is not strong enough to assert its claim to the traditional tolerance of Lebanon, where other stronger groups consistently infringe upon the religious peace with impunity. The party opposes Arab nationalism because it does not embrace all the Muslims in the world, and it proclaims the need for re-establishing an Islamic state.[55] The Liberation party in 1960 asked to be granted a license for political activity in Iraq under the system introduced by General Abdul Karim Kassem. The request was refused. However, another group of similar tendencies, the Iraqi Muslim party, was given a license.

The Iraqi Muslim party was formed under the same spiritual inspiration as the Muslim Brotherhood and the Liberation party. But no organizational connection seems to have existed between the different groups. The Muslim party attacked the Communists and also those in public office who supported communism in Iraq. It openly criticized the government for its pro-Communist leanings, which were evident until the events of Mosul and Kirkuk opened Abdul Karim Kassem's eyes. The Muslim party, in a memorandum to General Kassem, reproached the "leader" for having branded the Communists as "anarchists," thereby veiling the real nature of the "criminals." It asserted further that the illegal but powerful Communist party should be dissolved, the legal but powerless sham Communist party should be banned.

The Iraqi Muslim party urged the abolition of all laws not in accord with Islam, especially the laws of inheritance and the taxation of estates. The party's social program went directly back to the Koran and proclaimed: "Alms are a financial right of the poor." Its program advocated no social security legislation, therefore, but a distribution of alms according to the Islamic doctrine. The Muslim party adhered to the principle that women belong in the home, but that special educational facilities should be granted to them. The party aimed at a sort of presidential democracy supplemented by a popular referendum. In the field of foreign policy, the Iraqi Muslim party asked for unity of all Arab countries under the banner of Islam. Iraq should be considered a part of the Arab nation which could only be united on the basis of Islam. The united Arab nation should become the core of an Islamic nation comprising all the Muslims in the world. Pan-Arabism in the case of the Muslim party appears linked to Pan-Islamism. Concerning Israel, the party showed its violent side when it proclaimed in its program: "The problem of Palestine can only be solved by force."

There is no evidence that the Iraqi Muslim party ever mustered a great number of adherents. By December, 1960, all the leaders of the party had been thrown into jail by General Kassem, and the party has not re-emerged as a political force.

Of all the organizations which want to turn back the wheel of history, eliminate Western law and Western customs in favour of a return to the Koran, none is at the time of writing free to express its ideas and agitate for its ideals. Only the voice of the Association of the Ulemas in Algeria has not been completely silenced. All other groups, the Muslim Brotherhood, the Tahrir, and the Iraqi Muslim party, have been for all practical purposes banned from political life. The Islamic parties have not been able to gain support from more than a small minority of the people. But since they advocate or condone violence, they were and are considered dangerous antagonists by the various political regimes. What exists of genuine anti-Western feeling in the Arab world is expressed in the conservative Islamic movements.

Looking back at the reports of travelers in Arabic countries in the last century, for example Charles Doughty's *Arabia Deserta*, one may wonder that not more anti-Westernism remains in the Arab world of today. In fact, secularization has brought about the disappearance of the old antagonism founded on religious differences. What remains are spiritually and socially rootless masses whose emotions are easily directed by governments using modern mass media. One day these masses can be swayed against the West to destroy a United States Information Service (USIS) office; the next day they may hail a Western leader, if ordered to do so by their governments, without feeling any remorse about their contradictory conduct. In Iraq after the revolution of July 14, 1958, the political trend seemed to run irreversibly toward communism, but without much ado the direction was reversed following the massacres of Mosul and Kirkuk. While in Amman one year, the writer was stoned by gangs of unruly youths; the next year, everybody went out of the way to be friendly with the Westerner. The rules of mass behavior, applicable also in the Western world, determine the attitudes of the Arabs much more than do the spiritual complexes of older times.

6. *Christians and Muslims.* Assuming that Islam provides the foundation and cement of Arab unity, and that Pan-Islamism, in the personalities of Jamal ed-Din al-Afghani, Muhammad Abduh and Abdel Rahman al-Kawakibi gave birth to, or at least acted as midwife, to one brand of modern Arab nationalism, then a series of questions should be asked: How far is Islam still acting as motivating force? To what extent is Islam adjusting or adjustable to the demands of modern civilization? Where do non-Muslim Arabs stand in the development of Islam? And this question leads inevitably to a further incisive query: Is Arab nationalism possible without Islam? Is it possible without Arab unity?

To a visitor in the Middle East or in North Africa, it soon becomes evident that Islam has retreated from its former dominant position: it is no longer the be-all and end-all of all thought, but has declined to the point where it remains only one of several motivating forces in society. That does not exclude a great number, or even a majority, of people believing in the traditional creed and following its prescribed rites, but society, and especially its leaders, are no longer governed by religious laws and teachings. One might object that Islam has been declared the state religion by Arab countries from Mauritania in the west to Iraq in the east. Only Lebanon, which assumedly has a Christian majority (no census has been taken for over thirty years in order to keep this assumption intact and to preserve the religious-political peace), does not consider Islam the state religion. Since Islam has never created a "church" in the sense that the Orthodox, or Catholic, or Lutheran, or Episcopalian denominations have in Christendom, the problem of the relationship between "church" and state appears much less acute. There exists in Islam no administration or hierarchy comparable to the most numerous Christian groups. Furthermore, a special statute is automatically reserved for the religious minority under the ancient *millet* system, which accords "the peoples of the book" freedom to exercise their religion—as far as it does not disturb the majority belief, Islam—and guarantees them their separate laws of persons. This does not imply equality of Christians and Jews before the law in every sense, as is often claimed by nationalists. "As *dhimmis* [non-Muslims] they were subject to a tribute which comprised both land-tax (later termed *kharaj*) and poll-tax (later *jizyah*) but meantime enjoyed the protection of Islam and exemption from military duty. Herewith the principle of inequality between victor and vanquished—as long as the vanquished remained non-Moslem—was established as a permanent basis of policy."[56] Caliph al-Mutawakkil prescribed that Christians and Jews should only ride on donkeys, not on horses, that they should wear colored patches on their dress, apply distinctive signs to their homes, and keep their tombs level with the surrounding earth.

The feeling of having been discriminated against may have disappeared in the Christian upper classes, but it certainly still lingers on in the less privileged groups whose memories easily reach back a few decades to the time of Muslim rule, under which they were not granted equality. "Indeed, in many instances there is very serious trepidation. A great many Muslims are genuinely unaware of the insecurity and apprehension of their non-Muslim minorities. Many do not see the problem: it simply does not occur to them that non-Muslims would expect to be included in the group along with them. Others content themselves, though they do not content the minorities, by a serene assurance that 'Islam treats minorities well.' In any case, no Muslim group has cut across a Muslim society for a nationalist one; has substituted nationalism for Islam."[57] If this be true, then how is it that some Christians, especially in Lebanon, have come forward as fervent adherents of Arab nationalism?

Arab nationalism originally certainly meant something different to Christians than to Muslims. Some Middle Eastern Christians see nationalism as a secular movement. Arab nationalism does not mean Arab unity or Pan-Arabism to most Christians. They accept the Islamic background as part of a civilization in which they have participated since immemorial times, speaking the same language, living as separate *millets* in the same framework of laws. But few would go as far as Qustantin Zuraiq, a Christian professor at the American University, Beirut, who declares it the duty of every Arab to sanctify the memory of Muhammad and to interest himself in Islam.[58] The Christian intellectuals who took part in the first congress of Arab nationalists in Paris, 1904, believed in a secular society, in a division of religious and state affairs. Emerging from their close-knit *millets*, they desired to be integrated in a greater community, but not a community ordered according to the strict rules of traditional Islam. As members of a *millet*, their outlook was rather limited; few would have thought of a unitarian, centralized Arab state reaching from the Atlantic to the Indian Ocean. Their views seldom reached beyond the restricted horizons of the Middle East. They went as far as Egypt in the west, Iraq in the east, but scarcely to Morocco, the "Far West" of the Arab world. Arab Christians in their great majority remain in the limited sphere of local or regional nationalism. The bloody conflicts in Lebanon in 1958 and Iraq in 1959 showed the masses of Christians as opponents to integration in a Pan-Arab community. They prefer their traditional particularism to soaring plans of Pan-Arab— or even simply state-wide—unification.

To explain Arab nationalism in terms only of Pan-Arabism, to bring all the different forms of Arab nationalism under one hat would distort the picture as it develops in reality. Philip K. Hitti points out some of the principal variations in Lebanon:

The modern educated Moslems favored Pan-Arabism; the theologians leaned toward Pan-Islamism; the masses were conscious of no sharp distinction between the two 'Pan'-s. As for the Christians, they stressed Lebanese nationalism, although a number of the intellectuals were spokesmen for Arabism. Druzes also leaned toward Lebanese nationalism. The same could be said of Syria, where as late as 1955 a preacher in the Umayyad Mosque declared that to him an Indonesian Moslem was closer than the Christian prime minister of his country.[59]

The events of the last years in Lebanon and other countries have proved without doubt that there exists an Arab nationalism which does not care at all for Arab unification. Pan-Arabists try to deny to these local and regional nationalists the title of nationalists and denounce them as tools of colonialists, imperialists, feudalists, or whatever terms are currently in fashion in the modern demonology of the Arabs. In the struggle between the different nationalisms the Pan-Arabists have always to rely on the unity created by Muhammad and his immediate successors, while the particularists go farther back in history to prove the legitimacy of their aspirations. Since Islam remains, directly or indirectly, one of the principal factors of legitimation for the claim to re-establish full cultural unity and to create a state for all the Arabs, the direction Islam takes is crucial for the future direction of Pan-Arabism.

7. An Islamic Reformation? Two ways are obviously staked out for Islam: reformation or secularization. The reform movement initiated by Jamal ed-Din al-Afghani, Muhammad Abduh, and the Salafiyya seems to have lost its initial impulses and has bogged down for the time being. It is not enough to recall the former greatness of Islamic culture, to write pyramids of apologetic books on Islamic problems, to substitute apologetics for a critical historical analysis. But it is a fact, that the Muslim writers of today who want to liberate themselves from the strictures of apologetics must find a view of their own past in the writings of Westerners (Europeans and Americans). Nevertheless, observers like Wilfred Cantwell Smith or Jacques Berque see a renaissance of modern Islam.

Indeed, no Muslim transformation of the past hundred years is more striking than that from the quiescent passivity that led nineteenth-century observers to speak of the Islamic world (and even of Islam) as static and fatalist if not moribund, to the exuberant ferment of the present day . . . Modern Islam, whose renaissance has been more ebullient than thoughtful, and indeed has been aimed more at recapturing the vitality than at redefining the content or even the methods of faith.[60]

The reforming ferment after Afghani, Abduh, and Iqbal, described in the publications of Western Islamists remains, however, disappointingly slim. Ayub Khan, President of Pakistan, in his speech before the assembled *ulemas* of his country on May 3, 1959, pointed out some of the problems which assail Islamic society: "Looking forward was soon considered as an infraction against religion and looking backward as a proof of love towards one's religion. Every new progress, every new invention, every new teaching was suspected to be against Islam." And he admonished the *ulemas* to present Islam "in a language and in such a way that scientists experimenting in their laboratories, professors teaching at universities, farmers tilling their soil, workers toiling in the factories can understand this Islam without difficulty." In short, he appealed to them to adjust religion to the needs of modern society, somewhat in the spirit in which Kemal Atatürk had coined the slogan "modernize or perish" on his route toward total secularization of the state. The way open to reform of Islam is either return to the pure old doctrine, as advocated by the *salafiyya*, or revision through *ijma*. Von Grunebaum points out that in essential theological questions "the consensus of the learned yielded to the yearnings of the untaught," that furthermore "this *ijma* of the local learned is neither postulative nor normative; it is merely verifying, taking note that an agreement on a certain point actually does exist and by doing so making the material content of the agreement binding on the community."[61] According to the same author, *ijma* could well be used as an instrument of reform: "Yet to make *ijma* an active instrument of adjustment or even a tool of planned change, nothing is needed but a shift in public opinion sufficiently marked to compel its formal recognition by the learned in terms of a restatement of the nature of the consensus (which, were it to come, would unquestionably be experienced and presented as the discovery of its true and original character.)"

Not waiting for this new application of *ijma*, which would open the doors to reforms or adjustments of the Islamic doctrine, first the intellectuals, and then the masses, are turning away from religion altogether. If they feel the need for a new religion they may find it in the exaltation of nationalism or in the pseudo-rationalism of communism. To them nationalism provides truth; everything opposed to it is a lie. Nationalism acquires absolute value like the Koran—or the Bible. Into non-nationalist writings, consenting or inimical allegories are read by the exalted:

> Arabism is a quality given by our lands to their sons, like the shadow projected by a body to the earth. No definition in the world can change this. Arab nationalism—whatever its definition—takes roots in our unconscious, mixes with the smallest drops of our blood, and penetrates into the most intimate parts of ourselves. . . . We could be exterminated, but a new generation of Arabs would succeed us, as though born out of the same mold. And the songs of Arabism would arise again as always. . . . Nationalism is life. . . . That means that nationalism in our eyes represents a vital exigency. We cannot live without it, no other human society can.[62]

So chants the Iraqi poetess, Nazik al-Malaika. Again, she speaks—after heaven, hell:

> Colonialism attempts to turn us away from the benefits of nationalism as it has tried to prevent us gathering the fruits from our fortunate soil. This colonialism would steal our rivers, desiccate our mountains and our valleys, cut down the mulberry trees, the walnut trees, and the olive trees. . . . But our nationalism is the most precious booty which he desires for his robberies. If it were palpable,

they would have torn it from our hands: de Gaulle, Eisenhower, Macmillan, as they have wrenched from our hands our petrol, our gold, our cotton, our dates.

Religious fervor, a chiliastic promise, heaven and hell, salvation and perdition are all contained in this secular religion. Whoever has listened to the recitations of nationalist literati before their leaders, to harangues of agitators on the street corners, to the incitements of radio voices, and has seen the reactions to these sounds on the faces of the listeners, whoever has observed the reactions of men sitting around a loudspeaker, as their fathers once sat around a campfire, will be impressed, will never forget, the force of the incantations, the hope and hate, the elation and intoxication they cause. To the listeners, to the believers, this is for the moment a religion to be followed blindly. But it is a religion without God, a secular religion with fluctuating aims, with salvation within reach but never to be attained.

Turkey, more than any Arab country, has gone to the outer limits of secularization only to find that the masses will not always follow the leaders. Whenever and wherever they found a possibility, the conservative or reactionary masses coagulated around a group such as Celal Bayar's and Adnan Menderes' Democratic party, or around a personality like Marshall Cakmak, and forced them into the age-old conflict situation where Islam stands against secularization, religion against the Western way of life. The cleavage continues, profound as ever, and hampers progress. And no other Islamic country possesses such a large Western-oriented elite as Turkey. "The Turks are the one Muslim people in modern times who have generated a positive conception of what they want, and an operative loyalty toward attaining it," wrote Wilfred Cantwell Smith a few years ago. Events since the elections of 1957 lead one to doubt if Turkey has really passed over the mountains into the modern world, so attractively depicted by Atatürk. "Of the other Muslim peoples, the nationalist programs so far have either been purely negative, aimed at getting rid of something; or else they have proven unable to engender enough devotion to get themselves implemented," is the negative verdict of Wilfred Cantwell Smith.[63] Nationalist exaltation exempts neither the leaders nor the masses from dealing with the innumerable problems of both a material and a spiritual nature which assail them at the threshold of the modern technological world. "The drudgery of heroism" is hard to bear. And after attaining the principal goal, independence, the drabness of daily life seems unbearable to many, caused by evil conspiracies of the leaders or of foreigners. As Smith observes:

> Once one's group is free, the discipline to get up early in the morning, to work long hours, to turn down bribes, the inspiration to dream and the energy to actualize one's dreaming, all for national welfare and for national rewards, these have been less obvious. In the past, only Islam has provided for these peoples this type of discipline, inspiration, and energy. . . . Arab secularism . . . lacking the Greek or any philosophic basis, and lacking the Turkish practical commitment, tends to be simply an absence of all values, of life unsupported by conviction.[64]

Secularism has been branded as a Western import by Arab writers,[65] to which H. A. R. Gibb counters:

> It would, however, be absurd to regard secularism as a purely Western importation into the Muslim world. In every developed civilization, including the medieval Islamic civilization, secularism is to be found in a greater or less degree, whether open or concealed. Indeed the *ulema* themselves have contributed to the spread of secularism, for in the Muslim world it was mainly by the influence of the *Sufi* orders that the tendency to worldliness among the educated classes was counteracted; and in weakening that influence the *ulema* have not succeeded in putting any other influence in its place, except to the extent that they have co-operated in the new religious societies. . . . It was, therefore, into a house already swept bare that the secularizing influences from the West penetrated, through Western science, economics, and literature and through the dissolving effects upon the old social structure of secular education, of expand-

ing means of communication, of urban industries, and a host of other Western infiltrations. But it is remarkable that in the Arab world, unlike India, there has been little penetration of Western philosophy.[66]

Secularization sets in with the first pangs of Jacques Berque's "centrifugal curiosity," then spreads like a spot of oil in all directions; Westernization follows and finally the demand for reforms, the adjustment of ancient institutions to changed conditions. But nearly all reforms in the Arab world have been accomplished outside or against Islam.

3. The Quest for Unity

A. Pan-Arab Nationalism

Arab nationalism appears in different forms and it acts in many directions. Not even Pan-Arab nationalism is a uniform movement with a single goal, but rather a collective noun for partly contradictory expressions of national consciousness. It is not monolithic. Pan-Arab nationalism of yesterday may not be identical to Pan-Arab nationalism of today. Pan-Arab nationalism originates from the feeling, widespread in the Arab world, of belonging together, of being part of a great community held together by common language, history, law, and religion, in short of a cultural unit, the Arab nation. Elements of disunity or dissension are generally disregarded, the unity that once existed is projected into the present and the future. The Arab nation is assumed to exist already, at least since the Prophet Muhammad's time if not before his era. The presumedly existing nation seeks political expression: organization into one state. The mystique of Arab unity is so strong that all Arab leaders have to pay public homage to it—even when they are working against it. On the level of the intellectuals, the feeling of belonging together manifests itself in the desire for political unification; on the level of the masses, the same feeling is closely linked to the religious emotions. What appears as secular Pan-Arabism of the literate classes very often retains the cast of Pan-Islamism in the lower stratum of society. And on this lower level ancient religious cleavages and traditional antagonisms persistently work against the unifying forces.

There are several ways open for Pan-Arab nationalism to reach its postulated goal. It operates on the level of the people or through the governments. It choses persuasion, or elects to convert by force. It accepts the existing states—which have had most of their borders drawn by non-Arab powers—as sovereign entities, or denies them any historical legitimacy. Political unification takes precedence over personal freedom and social justice, or it is subordinated to the demands for individual liberty and social improvements. Depending on the ways and methods, the effects will be different and the results will vary. Pan-Arab nationalism is neutral as to the form of government, the economic system, and the social structures. It remains in the sphere of emotions rather than in the field of rational thinking. Reformers and demagogues have learned to play on these emotions, producing a variety of dissonant sounds.

Pan-Arab nationalism mythologizes Arab unity. As the German romanticists glorified the universal church and the universal Reich, so certain Arabs of today choose the medieval empires of the Umayyads and Abbassids as their ideal. They believe, *mutatis mutandis,* in the possibility of a *translatio imperii,* the transfer of imperial power from one people to another—in this case, from the all-powerful Arab caliphs of the seventh to the tenth centuries, to the renascent Arab nation of the twentieth century. While Otto von Freising's theory had to justify the transfer from Rome to Germany and to bridge the gulf in time and space and race, according to Arab feeling unity could bring about a resurgence of Arab power.

Pan-Arab nationalism recalls other "pan" movements, and one is tempted to find parallels. Pan-Germanism never managed to unite all peoples of Germanic tongues. Hitler tried to accomplish this feat by force, overpowering resistance by subversion and military might. His despotic rule discredited the idea of Pan-Germanism indefinitely.

Pan-Slavism won a certain ascendancy in Bohemia over politicians like Kramav, and in Bulgaria, Montenegro, and Serbia as long as the czars played their role as liberators of their Orthodox-Christian Slav brothers from the Turkish-Muslim yoke. The religious component in the nationalist independence movements in the Balkans was evident.

Pan-Turkism (often confounded with Pan-Turanism) has found some adherents outside of Turkey, within the Russian empire, where it would be rather unhealthy at the present time to express any such feelings. In republican Turkey, Pan-Turkism is advocated by an extreme right-wing minority, unable to form an influential organization since the movement was suppressed by President Ismet Inönü (at the time of writing Prime Minister in the second Turkish Republic) in 1944; but after the revolution of 1960 it gained ground again.

The Greek *megali idea* displays strong religious overtones. It was the Orthodox church which kept the Greek *millet* together under Turkish rule and first raised the flag of independence in 1821. Church leaders have fought in the forefront in all the struggles for liberation and unification into one sovereign state of all peoples of Greek tongue and Greek-Orthodox religion from Turkish or other alien rule. The goal has nearly been reached. Of all the Greek claims, only the one to northern Epirus or southern Albania is completely unfulfilled; Cyprus has achieved only independence instead of *enosis,* union with Greece, as demanded by the Greeks! But under what tremendous sacrifices all this has been attained. The Greek minorities in Bulgaria, Romania, and Russia have practically disappeared; the Greek colonies along the Aegean, the Mediterranean, and the Black Sea coasts of Anatolia, most of them between twenty-five hundred and three thousand years old, have been wiped out in the process of building a modern Greek national state.

The "pan" movements develop their own demonology. So has Pan-Arab nationalism. It snarls against alleged or real imperialists and colonialists, but its arch-enemy is Israel. In their desire to eliminate Israel as a sovereign state, Arabs of all persuasions find a unity of purpose. Unity in most instances is restricted to a few generalities, usually of a negative nature, such as the antagonism towards Israel. Observing the single-minded enmity of some Arab fanatics, one is reminded of the definition of a nation, proposed by two brilliant Englishmen: "A society united by a common error as to its origin and a common aversion to its neighbors."[1]

Pan-Arab nationalists accord exaggerated value to the idea of unity. Political unity takes precedence over all other objects in life. Problems seem to solve themselves when expanded over an enormous distance. "The Arab desire for unity is fundamentally a longing for normality, a determination to achieve a legitimate national right, a yearning for political health, and a desire for sounder economy and for greater stability and security in the Arab World."[2] Pan-Arab nationalism as such has developed no social and economic doctrine—Gamal Abdel Nasser, leader of one important faction of Pan-Arabists, the Baath party, and Ben Bella have tackled this task in different ways.

The defense of individual liberty occupies an extremely small place in the discussions of Pan-Arab nationalists. Freedom is neglected in the desire for unity. Unity is given such overwhelming importance that little thought is reserved for personal freedom. Their ideal of unity, a centripetal force of unfathomable strength, demands collective action, not guarantees of personal freedom and democratic rights. Like other "pan" movements, it tends to promote dictatorship rather than democracy. On one hand, the urgent solution of many local, social, and political problems is postponed because Pan-Arab nationalism absorbs all the strength of the elite in a certain area. On the other hand, Pan-Arab nationalism overexpands its forces, inflates its strength, and suffers an inevitable regression. For both tendencies Syria is a rather striking exemplar.

For the Arabs the dream of being united takes the place of Atatürk's more realistic but somewhat simple ideal of being "modern." Turkey was coerced into Westernization by a leader and an elite wielding dictatorial power. But the nation has reached a stage where the majority of the people think in terms of democracy without regard to the regime that governs them at the moment. Every regime since Atatürk justifies its rule by calling it democratic, or at least proclaims the restoration of democracy its principal aim. When individual rights were curtailed by Celal Bayar and Adnan Menderes, journalists and professors protested against the infringement of the right to free speech, students demonstrated in the face of overpowering police forces, and finally the officers rose in revolt and overthrew the arbitrary regime. Whatever the results, no other country in the Middle East has seen its elite rise against despotic power for freedom and for democracy. But demonstrations against alien powers and alleged lackeys of foreign states and for unity are daily occurrences in the Arab world.

All Arab countries, except the thin fringe of sheikhdoms and dwarf sultanates along the coast of the Arabian Peninsula from Aden to the Persian Gulf (the Arabs call it Arab Gulf) are free today. The old enemy, colonialism, has disappeared from all important parts of the Arab world. Neo-colonialism, this handy invention of the Soviet propaganda machine, in some areas takes the place of the old bogeyman—and always Israel remains if there is need to excite the masses. The dichotomy of anti-Western agitation and acceptance of Western civilization remains unbridged. While the Turks confer positive value on everything they aspire to, Arab nationalists tend to deride what they accept in daily life, namely Western ways and Western technology. A sort of cultural schizophrenia hampers their progress and creates unpredictable fluctuations in their political relationship to the West. As Ibn Khaldun points out, when events contradict the universal idea to which one would like them to conform, when analogies prove inexact and experience deceptive, then disillusionment sets in. The lack of distinction between partly existing cultural unity and postulated political unity, between what is and what should be, between the ideal and the reality, makes disillusionment inevitable. The result is *qalaq*, anxiety, and restlessness, Heidegger's feeling of *Geworfensein*, so typical for the Arab world.

The Arabs, who for centuries have been passive objects of history, now desire to become active subjects, or preferably one subject, of history. To achieve this aim they need to find appropriate methods and instruments. Pan-Arab nationalism must deal with the reality of the existence of different sovereign Arab states. It can either accept this reality, or try to transcend it. The first way is chosen by the oldest vehicle of Pan-Arab co-operation, the League of Arab States, the second by Gamal Abdel Nasser. The Arab League represents the aspiration of the disunited Arab states to unity. Gamal Abdel Nasser feels himself the representative of Arab unity as it exists and as it should be perfected. The assumedly existing Arab nation should, according to Pan-Arab nationalists, be endowed with a political organization which could take the shape of either a centralized state or a federation.

In the Arab world the nation has become—as it did in certain European countries—the object of a cult. To the nation pertains a *volonté générale* whose aim again is the attainment of unity. The nation is considered a living, supraindividual entity which wants to identify itself with a single state. The nation requires integration through political organization and representation to be lifted from the limbo of inactivity into the sphere of actual power. For the Pan-Arab nationalists, the nation is a natural spiritual unity, different from and superior to the sum of its parts, the individuals that compose it. Like Hegel, they believe in a *Volksgeist,* "a real quantity which operates in and on the individuals." But does this concept of the nation correspond to reality? Some doubts may be expressed:

> The ideology which conceives the people and the nation as supraindividual entities places itself in undisputable contrast to realities. It can neither do justice to the actual diversity of the people nor to the factual federal decentralization (U.S.A. and Switzerland). Instead of considering the people in its natural variety it exaggerates, parting from a specific politico-social situation, a unity, which exists

in certain respects, and takes this unity as its one and only characteristic. It does not take into account that a double function is inherent
in the representation of communities, namely integration—only representation makes the formation of a common will possible—and the
reproduction of something which already exists in reality. Integration means, if the represented is unreal, joining together to form a
unity; if the represented entity really exists, it signifies the adding
of personal, subjective elements by the representative, the transform-
ing of the represented content to the intellectual or spiritual level
of the representative. The people (*Volk*) appears, observed "from
the outside," as a unity . . . looked at "from the inside," (from the
subjective point of view of the members of the community) it is revealed rather as the sum of an infinite number of components, and
only after intensive reflection, or in case of immediate need of community support, the coherence is discovered or sensed. The people,
therefore, should be taken neither as a sum of isolated individuals nor
as a unit in a collectivist sense, because unity exists only under specific, more or less ephemeral, conditions.[3]

Weak cohesion of the people creates a qualitatively unsatis-
factory representation. The representatives reproduce on the political level interests and feelings of particular groups—family, clan,
tribe, army, religious or ethnic communities—and only a minority
of politicians represents a greater unit or the whole of the nation.
The tendency prevails to choose a dictatorial form of government
to overcome the dissensions. Authoritarian forms of government
offer the people support from outside themselves, provide them
with an ecto-skeleton of police-enforced rules and orders, while
democracy is based on the insights of the individual. Where the
centripetal forces which act within the individual are insufficiently
developed, there the call prevails for a "strong man" who is deemed
competent to re-establish order and represent unity. Since dissensions in the Arab world time and time again get the upper hand
despite, or because of, Pan-Arab nationalists' denying the very existence of conflicts, *zaïms* (leaders) are called in to re-create the unity
which in the Pan-Arab mind is already present.

The problem for the Arab world since the fall of the Ottoman

Empire is to establish a new society and new governments— Arab governments. How should the constituent power be formed? Old dynasties like the Hashemites offered themselves, but were only admitted in limited areas like Iraq and Jordan while they lost their homeland, Hejaz, to Ibn Saud. The intervention of foreign colonial powers, as well as emerging new classes, resisted the Hashemite claims to dynastic supremacy. Today we still find a number of rulers who base their power more or less openly on divine right. Neither the King of Saudi Arabia, the King of Jordan, the King of Libya, or the King of Morocco are constitutional monarchs in the European sense; their orders prevail over the written constitution. All, except Hussein of Jordan, who also claims descent from the family of the Prophet, combine religious office with secular power. General Fuad Chehab, from 1958 to 1964 President of the Lebanese Republic, the most democratic of the Arab states, is a descendant of the family that once ruled over Lebanon. He stands exactly at the point where traditional, charismatic, and democratic (rational) leadership meet.

To accept monarchs who claim to govern "by the grace of God," was one alternative in the formation of states. The other was to have the governmental system imposed by a colonial power. France and Britain transferred European systems of government to the Arab countries with all the paraphernalia developed since the time of the French revolution: constitution, bill of rights, division of powers, elections, parties, and other requisites of liberal democratic rule. What could not be imported was the common fund of ideas and beliefs which holds Western democracies together and forms a more or less firm basis for the working of democratic governments and the guarantee of liberty. Even in Lebanon, where parliamentary debate is unhampered to a degree that sometimes approaches anarchy, no government has ever fallen as long as the president of the republic held his protective hand over it, and no government has been dismissed by a vote of non-confidence of the legislature. Similarly, of the approximately fifty governments which have ruled in Iraq from 1921 to 1964, none was forced to resign by a regular parliamentary vote; they were forced out by "strong men," military juntas, popular demonstrations, or plain disintegration. One wonders how a democracy could function, when, for example, the head of the government in his tribal hierarchy remains subordinated to the chief of tribe, as was the case of the late Hazzaa al-Majali, killed in his office in Amman by an assassin's bomb in 1960. To acknowledge that the victor in an election has won by fair means, to recognize that the opposition is not composed of traitors but of loyal men of different opinion, requires a superhuman effort which few emerging peoples are willing to make.

With the advent of independence, the inherited Western constitutional systems were given a new interpretation and, in fact, emptied of their original sense. Leaders of genuine or doubtful charisma grasped power, new elites asserted their claim to rule. The officers corps emerged as the most powerful of the new elites. The officers were the first masters of modern technology which penetrated the Middle East and North Africa in the form of cannons and tanks. And the officers, more than civilian authority, disposed of the principal instrument of power, the army. Nothing is more ephemeral than the rule of *zaïms* and officers' juntas which have not acquired a firm basis of popular support. Since Arab unity and antagonism against colonialists and Israel are often the only problems in which a consensus of the people can be established, the leaders harp endlessly on these themes. No state can be founded on negative programs, no stable and lasting government can be constituted. Anti-Westernism is a weak cement for a modern state. The one positive point, the idea of Arab unity, seems as yet not sufficiently strong to guarantee permanent integration. The prime exemplar again is Syria.

While the Western constitutional structures were preempitied of their original content and one-man-rule established *de facto* or *de jure,* the old frame of political reference was attacked in a different direction. Nearly all the borders of the Arab states have been drawn by foreign powers. A look at a map shows the straight lines drawn by the victors in World War I. To what extent do the Arabs recognize these frontiers as their own? Shukry al-Kuwatly, President of Syria before union with Egypt and later First Arab Citizen by Abdel Nasser's grace, decries the lines dividing the states: "Our frontiers are not limits, they are wounds."

Pan-Arab nationalism rejects the state borders; its appeal cuts across the present frontiers. In its attack against barriers set up by foreigners it reaches down to deeper layers of Arab emotions, deeper than anti-colonialism. Most eastern Arabs share in the Bedouin mentality, of which the poets sang long before Muhammad's time. The Bedouin has no roots in any specific territory. His ideal of freedom is to rove unhindered over hundreds or thousands of miles of steppes and deserts in the Middle East and in North Africa. Even in recent times tribes like the Shammar used to graze their herds in four different states—Iraq, Syria, Jordan, and Saudi Arabia—disregarding the political borders. The Bedouin mentality, praised as the highest form of human spiritual development by Arab bards, exerts a strong hold over the farmers and the city dwellers in the Middle East. The rootless Bedouin of the desert finds his counterpart in the rootless masses of the modern cities. The Arab's feeling of unity transcends the limits set up by man. His loyalty is reserved to man, the leader of the family, the clan, the tribe, not to a certain state—which may be dominated by people he considers social or ethnic aliens. New loyalties had to be established after the disappearance of the Ottoman Empire. The period since World War I is characterized by the establishment of territorial states, a phase of development corresponding roughly to the seventeenth century in Western Europe. As feudal power is destroyed, allegiance is shifted from the lord to the land, from the person to a clearly and firmly delimited territory.[4]

Colonel T. E. Lawrence, the most famous hero of the British romanticists of the desert, observed the problems of state organization by the Arabs with some misgivings. In a conversation with Lowell Thomas, he said:

> History is against the probability of the creation of an Arabic Empire. The Semitic mind does not lean toward system or organization. It is practically impossible to fuse the diverse elements among the Semites into a modern, closely knit state. On the other hand, the Semites have been more fertile in ideas than any other people. The Arabian movement has presented itself to me as the latest expression of the influence of the desert upon the settled peoples; the Semitic spirit has again exercised its influence over the Mediterranean basin. . . . The desert seems to produce only one idea, the universality of God. We who have gone out to discover the meaning of the desert have found only emptiness; nothing but sand, wind, soil, and empty space.[5]

The Arabs indeed have not built an empire but a number of sovereign states—fourteen at the time of writing have been admitted to the United Nations. Nearly every one of these states has, in the past, paid lip service to Arab political unity, but when the delegates gather at the meetings of the League of Arab States, sometimes the consensus does not even suffice to publish a noncommital final communiqué about unity of purpose. The rifts between the Arab countries are too well known to be retraced on these pages; whenever one conflict is stilled, another opens. In the middle, one always finds Egypt, which has a different conception of Arab politics than most of its neighbors.

B. *The League of Arab States*

Even Pan-Arab nationalists are of divided opinion on the best way to accomplish unity; whether to form a confederation of sovereign states (*Staatenbund*), a federation or federal union in which each state would renounce part of its sovereignty but keep its separate identity (*Bundesstaat*), or to join closely in a single centralized state. There is obviously a wide difference between the three systems, but Arabs tend to mix all forms of Pan-Arabism. From two sides, attempts have been made to bring the ideal of Arab political unity nearer to realization. On one side the League of Arab States provides a vehicle for co-ordination of policies and, if desired by all, unification. The Arab League has never been considered a strong organization. The types of government of the member states run the gamut from medieval theocracy to "comfortable anarchy" in Lebanon, which lives according to Thomas Jefferson's principle that the least government is the best government.

Decisions are only binding for those states which have voted for them, and even in this case there exists no control over the application of the resolution. Looking for historical parallels, one is reminded of the projects for a League of Italian States banded around during the Risorgimento by heads of state from Naples, Rome, Florence, Vienna, and Paris, and even reflected in the Treaty of Zürich. A more recent parallel would be the Council of Europe, to which Abdel Khalek Hassouna, General Secretary of the Arab League, compares his organization. The Arab League has often been branded as a tool of Egyptian power politics, especially since its first and its present general secretaries are Egyptian diplomats. Some of the criticisms against it are unquestionably well founded. But under prevailing conditions it seems rather astonishing how much independence the Arab League has retained under the leadership of Hassouna, an accomplished diplomat. Many disputes between Arab countries are ironed out in the framework of the League, whose representatives must show the patience of Job in dealing with its unruly members. Its usefulness was clearly revealed in August, 1958, when the warring factions of the League suddenly found a common basis of agreement in reaffirming their adherence to the principles of the League, while the members of the United Nations, which had become the tiltyard of Arab strife, looked on in happy disbelief as the conflicts seemed to disappear in the thin air of a unanimous resolution. Two years before, Anwar as-Sadat, one of the closest collaborators of Gamal Abdel Nasser, had declared: "The Arab League is dead!"[6] The new Egypt in 1958 was glad to take the slow boat of the Arab League out of the dispute.

On this occasion Article 8 of the pact was reaffirmed, which proclaims that every member state agrees to respect the system of government established in the other member states, considering such system the exclusive right of each state, and promises also to abstain from any action tending to change the regime. This principle of non-intervention would guarantee the existence of separate Arab states and channel the desire for unity into democratic grooves where the interests of each separate country would be safeguarded. It does not hamper common action if so desired. That little in this way has been accomplished should not be blamed on the pact but on the policies pursued by the member states. The "regrouping of the Arabs" which, according to Abdel Khalek Hassouna,[7] is the *raison d'être* of the League, may not have made much headway. But the Arab League has proved its value as a clearing house of ideas for Arab co-operation and as a place where disputes may be ironed out. Here is not the place to trace step by step the failures and accomplishments of the League; that it still exists in the face of criticisms and dissensions proves its value. If it reflects more often the diversities than the unity of the Arab world, it is because this corresponds in fact to Arab reality. Separated by deserts, divided by centuries of divergent development, medieval and modern governments meet at the same table to solve problems which to every one of them appear in a different light. The question arises under the circumstances whether unity or disunity appears more natural. The transfer of the principle of unity from the metaphysical to the real remains an obstacle nearly impossible to overcome.

The Arab League can survive and accomplish its aims only as long as it remains true to its charter, as long as it upholds the principles of equal rights and of free debate. Whenever it strays from this clearly outlined path, it loses influence and falls into one of its recurrent eclipses. It cannot fulfil all expectations, because its weaknesses are the compounded weaknesses of its members. But to have a forum set up for the free expression of ideas seems of no little value. If it is perverted and used for ulterior purposes by some of its members, then this shows up the obliquities of Arab politics.

C. Nasserism

Gamal Abdel Nasser provides the antithesis to the Arab League's approach to Arab unity. Abdel Nasser has become the paladin of Pan-Arab nationalism; he is identified by many in the West, as in the East, as the personification of the quest for Arab unity. But Abdel Nasser has no monopoly of Arab nationalism, not even a monopoly of Pan-Arab nationalism. Other forces in addition to Nasser work for Arab unity, some with democratic means. Other Arabs pursue different aims, and they are not less nationalist, in their own way, than the Egyptian leader. Allal el-Fassi, Mehdi ben Barka, and Mahjoubi Aherdane in Morocco, Ahmed ben Bella, and Habib Bourguiba are all Arab nationalists. Is Pierre Gemayel[8] in Lebanon less of a nationalist than Saeb Salem? Or why should Nuri as-Said in Iraq be excluded from the list? He fought with arms against the Turkish overlords before some of the present leaders were even born. True, these men represent different forms of nationalism; but there is no reason why the term "Arab nationalism" should be reserved exclusively for Gamal Abdel Nasser's brand.

Abdel Nasser appears to many Arabs as the man of providence. He is no doubt a charismatic leader who exerts a great amount of personal charm even on Western visitors. His family life inspires confidence. And he conveys the impression that he agrees in principle with his interlocutor's ideas while he pursues his own ideals. Many visitors consider him a reasonable man.

In the Arab mind, however, a different picture of Abdel

Nasser emerges. He is hailed as a giant, a hero, a superman.[9] He is identified with archetypes of Arab myths and history. Age-old conceptions of salvation and redemption are revived and mix with modern ideas of progress and liberation. He seems to promise a return to glorious times, the renaissance of the Arab Empire in all its glamour. He is the incarnation of Arab self-assertion. For the believers, Abdel Nasser is more than a politician, he represents their dreams. Failures cannot diminish his hold on the masses, because their adherence is not based on reality.

Abdel Nasser's weapon is not the sword but the word. He may not be quite up to the highest standards of Arab rhetoric, but his propaganda machine in Cairo finds no competition. A Syrian Communist once told this writer that he would rather hear the mellifluous "Voice of the Arabs" than the pedestrian exhortations from Moscow. The word to the Arab is reality, and reality is the word. The connection of word and fact, so important to Western thinking, may be discarded in the Arab world; or rather, the facts must conform to the word and not vice versa.[10]

Radio Cairo, the "Voice of the Arabs," and the "Voice of Palestine," pour out a steady stream of words in support of Abdel Nasser. His enemies, alleged or real, are vilified in terms not heard since Goebbels' and Hitler's ignominious deaths. The largest propaganda machine this side of Moscow appeals to the Arabs to overthrow their governments, to get rid of their feudal lords, of the colonialists and the lackeys of colonialists. In times of highest tensions, appeals for the assassination of opponents like King Hussein of Jordan are broadcast without reticence. The vocabulary of abuse pours forth in the full richness of the Arab language. This propaganda is directed not only toward Arabs but toward the entire Islamic world and toward Black Africa, the three circles of activity outlined in Gamal Abdel Nasser's *Philosophy of the Revolution.* Western statesmen do not escape abuse: the former socialist Prime Minister of France, Guy Mollet, is accused of having been a spy in Hitler's service in 1942-43.

The violence with which opponents are attacked reveals another trait of Abdel Nasser's character. Whenever failure threatens, he resorts to violence. He writes: "It was easy then, and I still find it easy now, to shed the blood of ten, twenty, or thirty persons in order to strike fear and panic in the hearts of many hesitants, and thus force them to swallow their passions, their hatred, and their whims. But what result could such an action achieve?"[11] Abdel Nasser condoned the concentration camps set up in Egypt, the torture chambers of his Heydrich, Abdul Hamid Sarraj in Syria, the abductions, terrorism, assassinations, and the incitements to revolution in neighboring states emanating from Syria in the heyday of the United Arab Republic. The excesses of Abdel Nasser's henchmen cannot be excused as youthful nationalist exuberance or denied as malevolent inventions of colonialists and Zionists. Too many are the cases, too many the proofs. Violent was Abdel Nasser's reaction to the refusal of American credits for the Aswan High Dam, violent was his reaction after the killing of Patrice Lumumba in the faraway Congo, whose death was taken as an excuse to nationalize Belgian assets in Egypt.

Abdel Nasser once lamented that the masses did not follow the vanguard of the revolution:

> The vanguard performed its task; . . . it forced Farouk to abdicate and stood by expecting the mass formations to arrive at their ultimate object. It waited and waited. Endless crowds showed up, but how different was the reality from the vision! The multitudes that arrived were dispersed followers and disparate remnants. . . . We needed discipline but found chaos behind our lines. We needed unity but found dissension. We needed action but found nothing but surrender and idleness.[12]

How different is the tone now, twelve years later. Abdel Nasser identifies himself with the masses. He is the people. The people has accomplished the revolution of July 23, 1952. Since he is the people, his regime is a democracy. We find here the same "absorptive representation" as in many other better known dictatorships. The people act exclusively through their leader. There may be plebiscites and elections, but the people are not given a chance to change regime or to alter the orders of the leaders. The decision to delegate all power to the leader, which is imputed to the people, is irrevocable. While in Western democracies the will of the citizens often differs from that of their representatives —as proved in many a referendum or in public opinion polls—in Egypt, as in other dictatorships, it is now blandly assumed that the leader always and forever expresses the desires of the people. There is no choice, no possibility to check whether the alleged identity of will and aims really exists. That Abdel Nasser does not want to be elected to a life term as president does not mean that an opponent of the regime could be chosen. The leader monopolizes the expression of the will of the people, he absorbs all representative functions through which the will of the citizens could be actualized. In the West this is not called democracy, but despotism.

In his five-and-a-half-hour speech of May 21, 1962, before the National Congress of Popular Forces, in which he outlined his socialist charter for the United Arab Republic, Abdel Nasser professes his creed in the necessity of a revolution:

> The Revolution is, in fact, the only means by which the Arab nation can be freed from the fetters which oppress it. . . . The Revolution is the only means to compensate for the delay imposed on the Arab nation; this delay was a natural consequence of oppression and exploitation. . . . The revolutionary vanguard action must be undertaken by the popular revolutionary commands in the United Arab Republic which . . . must assume the responsibilities of the heart-land with respect to the determination to realize liberty, socialism, and unity in the Arab Nation.[13]

Reading the text of Abdel Nasser's oration two points stand out: First, he vows to accomplish a revolution and second, he is ready to use revolutionary methods. The League of Arab States, on the contrary, considers itself an instrument of peaceful evolution. Abdel Nasser's revolution is not confined to Egypt but should be extended to the whole Arab nation, and that means to all the other Arab states. Equalizing social conditions would pave the way to Arab unity. "The responsibility of the United Arab Republic to insure progress, to consolidate and protect it, extends to the whole Arab Nation."[14] Common language, common history, and common expectancies are the features which prove the unity of the Arab nation, according to Abdel Nasser. He has an upside down Hegelian conception of this unity: "The existence of these divergences is in itself a proof for the unity. These divergences are born out of the social struggle which takes place inside the Arab reality." Unity (thesis) creates disunity (antithesis) which is proof of unity (sythesis) . . . . Abdel Nasser continues: "Unity of the objective must constitute the slogan for Arab unity in the moment of passing from the phase of political revolution to social revolution. The slogan which served in a previous stage of the national struggle, namely the stage of the political revolution against imperialism, must be rejected." And he adds a promise of peaceful methods: "Unity must not be imposed. . . . Therefore, constraint in all its forms is an action contrary to unity. . . . Arab unity in no way implies a uniform constitutional form which must ineluctably be applied; it is rather a long way in which the stages and forms may multiply before the final objective is attained."[15]

What Abdel Nasser has in mind is obviously a sort of "Arab socialism in one country" from which it would spread to the other parts of the Arab nation. For this purpose the Egyptian leader intends to set up a federation of popular movements, a Nasserist International. Al-Ahram on April 11, 1962, had promised that Egypt would "never sacrifice Arab unity for self-progress"; now socialism takes precedence over unification. Abdel Nasser stresses his allegiance to the League of Arab States, "because, even if it is not able to lead the Arab race to its noble and faraway objective, it is able, at least, to advance some steps on this way."[16]

If Abdel Nasser would not stray from the principle of non-intervention set down in the pact of the Arab League and from the peaceful proclamation of May 21, 1962, the way to progress of the Arab world would be greatly enhanced. But, meanwhile, the Egyptian propaganda machine continues to vilify certain Arab leaders, sowing hatred and inciting the populations to revolt.

The approach to the Syrian problem shows Abdel Nasser again as an empiricist and pragmatist. He adjusts his policies and changes his methods according to the resistance he meets or the support he gains. His doctrines are not immutable. Nasserism without Nasser would not be the same. He is the charismatic leader who continually explores new possibilities, who electrifies the masses and awakens their innermost hopes and expectations. He alone commands a mass following. His social program may or may not work, but Abdel Nasser's sway over the people seems to depend only to a limited degree on his programs' success or failure. The striking reversals he has suffered have not undermined his position, because Arab allegiances transcend reality.

At present the socialism of Nasser is increasing the cleavage which separates Egypt from some of the other Arab countries. To overcome this uncomfortable position, which does not correspond to Egyptian ambitions, Abdel Nasser sponsors "common markets" patterned more or less on the European Economic Community. The formation of an "African common market" was agreed upon by the signatories of the treaty of Casablanca, the United Arab Republic, the Algerian Republic, Morocco, Guinea, Mali, and Ghana, which on June 16, 1962, extended their co-operation by concluding a military pact and organizing a united military command under the Egyptian general, Muhammad Fawzi. This pact was dissolved according to the decisions of the Organization of African Unity, founded in May, 1963, in Addis Ababa. A second common market treaty was signed in July, 1962, by the United Arab Republic, Syria, Kuwait, Jordan, and Morocco with the aim of building a counterweight to the European Economic Community whose tariff policies are felt as a threat to their interests by a number of extra-European states not associated with this organization. The African and the Arab common markets reflect again Abdel Nasser's interest in two circles in which Egypt, according to his vision, should be the core.

Pan-Arab and Pan-African tendencies in Egypt's foreign policy are complemented by "positive neutralism" and non-alignment. Both are made possible by Soviet tactics, derived from Lenin's recipe, of collaboration with national-bourgeois movements of liberation. Russian support enables Abdel Nasser—and other rulers—to play East against West and profit from both sides' aid. Soviet aid seems not unconditional. Arriving in Cairo on March 10, 1964, the Soviet leader declared: "We wholeheartedly acclaim the Arab people's movement for unity on an anti-imperialist, anti-colonialist basis."[17] And six days later, in Aswan, he enlarged on the same theme. Jay Walz, correspondent of the *New York Times,* summed up Khrushchev's thoughts: "In Aswan . . . the Soviet Premier said Arab leaders should be less interested in nationalist unity and more eager to get the workers of the world to unite. 'I have heard your leaders urge Arabs to unite,' declared Mr. Khrushchev to his Aswan audience. 'In such a case, what shall we Russians here do? Go home?' "[18]

The great powers' acquiescence permitted Abdel Nasser first to send troops to Syria before and during the union between the two countries, to dispatch a strong expeditionary force to Yemen, and to transport substantial military aid to Algeria during its border conflict with Morocco. Abdel Nasser's neutralism is definitely lopsided, favoring the Soviets over the West, as is clearly shown by the votes in the United Nations, by the declarations of neutralist conferences, and by actions in the Middle East and Africa. In his programmatic speech before the Congress of Popular Forces there was no end to Nasser's attacks against the West, while both Soviet imperialism and communism remained exempt from criticism. Abdel Nasser, however, is not a Communist. His projects are a mixture of nationalism and socialism—an ominous combination, as recent history has shown.

In his Charter of Arab Socialism, his third attempt to institutionalize the revolution and provide it with a solid political-juridical foundation, Abdel Nasser promises to overcome the class struggle waged by feudalists against the underprivileged. He pledges a better distribution of riches and a continuation of agrarian reform, not by nationalization of the land but by extension of agrarian credits and promotion of co-operatives. Industrialization is declared one of the principal goals; the aim is to build up heavy industry without neglecting increased production of consumer goods. All sectors of the economy should be developed according to a central plan. Part of production is already nationalized, part would remain free, providing a field for private investments. Progress, progress, progress becomes the keynote of all planning—technological progress in a Western sense, but rejecting the underlying intellectual foundations which made the technological revolution in the West possible. The national income should be doubled every ten years—an ambitious goal.

How Arab socialism will work in practice nobody can say yet. Part of the profits of nationalized industries is handed out in the tradition of Islamic charity to the employees, instead of being reserved for urgently needed new investments. The nationalizations since 1961 discouraged private investments and chased away foreign interests. Foreigners—Greeks, Italians, Swiss, Lebanese—who have lost their enterprises continue to leave the country in droves. This does not mean that Egyptians are unable to fulfil the tasks until recently accomplished by foreigners, but the impoverishment in material and intellectual fields is all too obvious.

Abdel Nasser has the enormous advantage of ruling over what is probably the most docile population on earth. The fellahin of the Nile Valley have seen many conquerors and many regimes come and go. Revolts have hardly more than scratched the surface of the inert masses. Their development is measured by centuries, not by decades. How many popular upheavals, not merely palace revolutions, have occurred in the last six thousand years of Egyptian history? Is there any place where art has changed so little over so long a stretch of time, from the earliest Pharaoh to the Hellenistic and Roman eras? It takes a long period to let the agitation of the citified lower middle class, which dominates present-day Egypt, filter down to the fellahin and stir them out of their traditional ways. The rebellion of Sheikh Muhammad al-Ghazali against the proposed equality of women with men, and the demonstration of the students of al-Azhar University in support of their venerated teacher after the proclamation of the socialist charter may only be a rearguard action of reactionaries, but they are also symbolic for the forces resisting Abdel Nasser's dreams. Since the beginning of his reign Abdel Nasser finds—his continuous assertions to the contrary—support in the maligned West. When the Free Officers squashed King Farouk's corrupt regime and instituted reforms, Abdel Nasser was hailed for his efforts to clean up Egypt. "Puritans of the Nile" remained for years a catchy label, invented not in Cairo but in London. Banning of prostitution and of the Twist, admonishments to women not to wear lipstick[19] are requisites of nearly any modern authoritarian regime. But moralizing is not identical with morality.

Whether Abdel Nasser's nationalism or his socialism or any other brand of nationalism or socialism in the Arab world will prevail, only the future can tell. Meanwhile developments recall Lord Acton's famous words: "For history is often made by energetic men, steadfastly following ideas, mostly wrong, that determine events."[20]

D. Arab Versions of Socialism

Socialism has become the fashionable political costume of the underdeveloped countries. What goes for socialism in Asia and Africa often is unrecognizable to Western socialists used to thinking in terms of a specific ideology. Abdel Nasser's socialism is not the only socialism in the Arab world; other movements vie with his for the allegiance of the masses. Some of them, such as Kamal Jumblat's socialism in Lebanon, can be disregarded as political forces outside of their local range. Jumblat wins his seat in parliament, not because he claims to be a socialist, but because as a member of a leading family of Druses he can count on the fealty of some of his coreligionists. The party of the late Antun Saadeh, which agitates for Greater Syria and launched the coup in Lebanon on New Year's Eve of 1961, also proclaims itself socialist—national-socialist in this case. The title of National-Socialist party was used by Suleiman Nabulsi's organization in Jordan, ousted by King Hussein from the government during the upheaval of April, 1957. Habib Bourguiba in Tunisia also labels his regime "Socialist."

In Morocco, Ahmed Reda Guedira, King Hassan's trusted right-hand man, formed in 1964 a Democratic Socialist party. A few years earlier he had named his first political organization Liberal party, and later he had founded a Front for the Defense of the Constitutional Institutions. The political trend from an imitation of liberalism to socialism shows clearly in the change of names. More seriously socialist is Mehdi ben Barka's National Union of Popular Forces, one of the opposition parties in Morocco, which is one of the few Arab countries that still preserves the multiparty system.

One of the most far-reaching experiments in socialism was started under the leadership of Ahmed ben Bella in Algeria after the liberation. Before the country was even given a constitution, the "vacant" farms, shops, and industries (left by the mass exodus of the French), were expropriated by the Algerian Republic and administered under a system called "*autogestion*."[21]

This "self-administration" appears as the most original feature of the Algerian revolution; its model can be found in Tito's Yugoslavia. A general assembly of the permanently employed workers meets every three months. It decides the general lines along which affairs shall be conducted and elects a workers' council and a directing committee of three to eleven members. A manager, who represents the state and the nation and who is nominated by the government on the advice of the municipal council for self-administration, executes the decisions of the general assembly and the workers' council and directs everyday business. A municipal council in each township, consisting of the chairmen of the directing committees of the self-administered enterprises, one representative each of the party, the trade unions (UGTA—*Union générale des travailleurs algériens*), the army, and the municipal authorities, helps expand and develop the "*autogestion*." A national plan shall provide the general direction for all economic activity.

The constitution,[22] accepted by a great majority of Algerians in the referendum of September 8, 1963, provides for a mixed economic system in which elements of state administration and self-administration co-exist with remainders of private enterprise. It attempts a conciliation between Islamic tradition and socialism. The preamble to the constitution states: "Islam and the Arab language were the efficient forces of resistance against the attempts of the colonial regime to de-personalize the Algerians. . . . Algeria must assert that the Arab language is the official and national language and that it takes its main intellectual strength from Islam."

The party program accepted in April, 1964, proclaims: "Algeria is an Arab-Muslim country. . . . The division of the Arab world into individualized geographical and economic units could not relegate to a secondary role the elements of unity forged by history, the Islamic culture, and a common language. . . . The Algerian revolution must give back to Islam its true face, the face of progress. . . . The Algerian culture shall be national, revolutionary, and scientific. 1) Its role as national culture shall consist in the first place in rendering to the Arab language, which is the expression of the cultural values of our country, its dignity and its efficiency as a language of civilization. . . . In this way it [the language] will fight cultural cosmopolitanism and the occidental impregnation."[23]

While asserting the values of Islam and the Arab language as unifying forces, the party program is clearly based on a Marxist conception of history, and it recommends the application of Marxist methods. It justifies the one-party system and "democratic centralism" as used by the Communist parties all over the world. It calls for a class struggle against the big and small bourgeoisie, against small and big farmers, against "exploiting private property" and a fight against the multi-party system. The program promises further land reform and industrialization, to lift the nation out of the doldrums of widespread unemployment and underdevelopment.

Comparing this program with President Ahmed ben Bella's inaugural speech[24] of April 16, 1964, to the party congress of the National Liberation Front, one recognizes a difference of tone. The program appears in its substance more radical and dogmatic. Ben Bella, while violently threatening to exterminate all opposition, had to take into account that other motivations move many Algerians, that contrasting forces are active in the nation, and that a complete consensus about the aims to be pursued is still lacking. The president's speech, therefore, was not dogmatic but followed the self-set rules of his *"empirisme orienté"* (directed empiricism). In the leading "socialist élite" of Algeria a struggle is going on between groups following the Marxist ideology and others adhering—be it out of conviction or only for tactical purposes—to Islamic tradition.

While the Algerian National Liberation Front has gone far in applying socialist principles, the Arab party which first started and has gone farthest in elaborating a socialist ideology, is undoubtedly *hizb al-ba'th al-arabi al-ishtiraki* or, more simply, Baath, headed by Michel Aflaq, a Christian and former Communist. Comparing the program of the Baath party with Abdel Nasser's socialist charter, one cannot fail to see the striking resemblance between the two. The Baathists were prime movers for Syria's *Anschluss* in 1958, which was achieved due to Syrian initiative. They believed that they could give the Egyptian revolution a social content it

101

sorely lacked. Some of the leading Baathists—but not Michel Aflaq —accepted high posts in the government of the United Arab Republic, but were never given a real function. They sat in their Cairo offices and saw real power slipping away from them. In the well-prepared elections for the National Union, which should have given Abdel Nasser's revolution an organizational support, the Baath party received only an infinitesimal number of representatives and was practically eliminated from political influence in Syria. Instead of collaboration with the Baathists, the Egyptian *raïs* used police power to keep Syria in step. His henchman was the all-powerful chief of police, minister of the interior, and finally chief of government in the "Northern Province," Abdul Hamid Sarraj. For a while Abdel Nasser attempted to push even Sarraj out of his dominating position by sending an Egyptian proconsul, his friend Marshall Abdul Hakim Amer, to Syria. The Egyptian, however, with his different mentality did not get along well with the Syrians, and finally had to leave quietly, recognizing the failure of his mission. This left Sarraj as relatively independent satrap of Syria, where he established the worst police regime this side of the Iron Curtain. A second Egyptian attempt to oust him, by promoting him and drawing him to Cairo, succeeded, but it left the field open for the *Putsch* of September 28, 1961, which led to the secession of Syria from the United Arab Republic.

In this struggle for power the Baathists were involuntary onlookers. Their attempt to contribute their program to Abdel Nasser's Pan-Arabist revolution had failed while they were under the Egyptian's rule. But after Syria's secession, they now see many of their important claims and plans fulfilled in Cairo. Abdel Nasser, with an age-old political trick, is stealing the wind out of the Baathists' sails.

The Baath party's program[25] is imbued with a high sense of mission. It wants before all to achieve "the unity and freedom of the Arab nation." "The Arabs are a single nation, having a natural right to exist within a single state and to be free to realize all its potentialities," proclaims the "constitution" of the party. "The Arab nation is characterized by an eternal mission which manifests itself in the form of a complete regeneration through the stages of history, leading to the reformation of human existence, the advancement of human progress, and the enhancement of harmony and co-operation among nations." This idea of a special mission of the Arab nation in the development of mankind is based on a somewhat Hegelian conception of history, and while the historical assumptions on which the Baathist theories are founded undoubtedly contain a good deal of imagination, the logic is better than in Abdel Nasser's charter.

Revolution is the means by which the Baath party wants to reach its goals: "The Arab Resurrection Socialist party is revolutionary, believing that its principal goals of reawakening Arab nationalism and building socialism cannot be achieved except by revolution and strife." This sounds very aggressive, and knowing the mild personality of Michel Aflaq one may be astonished at the tone of the party's pronouncements. But often the gentle introvert when sallying forth from his ivory tower uses power more ruthlessly than any other man. Another "socialist," Kamal Jumblat, sent his vassals into bloody combat against the pro-government forces during the revolution in Lebanon in 1958, while mouthing declamations of Ghandi-type non-violence.

Socialism, according to the Baath party, "will permit the Arab people to realize its own potentialities." The party feels that "socialism will cause the Arab genius to unfold in the most complete manner." According to the party program, socialism implies the redistribution of real estate, including a land reform, the nationalization of public utilities, transportation, large-scale industries and "enterprises based on great natural resources," obviously meaning oil. "All (relevant) foreign companies and concessions are to be abolished." Besides the nationalized sector, an area of free enterprise is retained. The whole economy should be regulated according to a state plan. The state also provides social security to the population and organizes all cultural and educational institutions according to the demands of Arab nationalism; this amounts to state culture in a totalitarian sense.

The Baath party guarantees in its "constitution" individual rights and democratic principles. However, it shows little understanding for the ethnic and religious minorities who live in the Arab world. Arabic would be the official language of the state and all the citizens. "It alone is recognized in correspondence and in teaching." Kurds and Turkomans, Armenians and Berbers, therefore, would be denied any official use of their languages. All denominational, factional, tribal, parochial, or regional loyalties would be wiped out. "Full rights of citizenship will be bestowed upon every citizen living in the Arab homeland who identifies himself solely with the Arab homeland and dissociates himself from every racial group." Short shrift is made with dissenters, who are threatened with expulsion: "Whoever agitates on behalf of, or is connected with, a racial group opposed to the Arabs, or whoever immigrates into the Arab homeland, for the purpose of colonization, will be expelled from the Arab homeland."

Abdel Nasser in his speeches and in his socialist charter repeatedly refers to God, and he even attempts to prove that socialism is in accordance with the Koran and Hadith, the Islamic tradition. The Baath program on the other hand does not mention God or Islam, it appears completely secular. Only where it prohibits the lending of money at interest does it reach back to Islamic teachings —but this could also refer to Marxist theory.

In quick reversals, so typical of Arab history, the Baathists, allied with part of the armed forces and with admirers of Abdel Nasser, overthrew the regime of General Kassem on February 8, 1963, in Baghdad, and on March 8, 1963, the government of Khaled al-Azm in Damascus. In the following months the Baathists squeezed the Nasserists out of all the positions of power in both countries. While the struggle between the two main groups of Pan-Arab nationalists became more and more violent, the early attempt to form a triple union between Iraq, Syria, and Egypt collapsed. It would be an exercise in futility to enumerate all the uprisings and the swings of the political pendulum back and forth between the poles of union and separation. Worse than the political upheavals are the struggles going on in the minds of the people.

The Baath, ruling in Syria and Iraq, appeared unable to keep its promises and to fulfil its program. Its economic policy met with no success, and its Pan-Arabism proved a failure since all moves to achieve an understanding with Abdel Nasser broke down. Under the stress of governing two unruly countries, the fight against the autonomist Kurds, for which Syrian troops were sent to Iraq's aid, and the inability to further the union of the Arabs, the Baath split into different factions. Already in the late 1950's Abdallah Rimawi, former Minister of Foreign Affairs in Jordan, had thrown in his lot with Abdel Nasser. Akram Haurani, former Vice President of the United Arab Republic, broke with Michel Aflaq, taking with him his personal clientele in Hama, the political nucleus of the Socialist party, which he had brought as a wedding gift into the Baath party when the two movements merged. In Iraq a radical faction under Ali Saleh as-Saadi failed to grasp power over the party and the state. A double *Putsch* on November 13 and 18, 1963, led to the ousting first of the radical wing, then of all the Baathists, from the Iraqi government while President Abdul Salam Muhammad Aref enhanced his own power. The fratricidal struggle spread from Baghdad to Damascus and Beirut and left the Baath, which had never represented more than a minority of the people, weakened. In Lebanon the Baath is officially banned, but tolerated by the authorities. In Syria at the time of writing it is still hanging on to power with the support of high-ranking army officers. Hassan E. Saab, a Lebanese writer, states in an article under the headline "Syria submits to socialism without believing in it": "Since Abdel Nasser ruled Syria, every time a party takes power in Damascus, its first aim is to proclaim itself socialist. And every time socialism is applied with vigor, invisible forces emerge out of the dark to destroy the man, the party, or the regime who try to impose social-ism on the Syrians. Therefore, to many theoreticians, socialism appears in a country like Syria as a doctrine against nature."[27]

The activities of the Baath are mainly restricted to the Middle East. In North Africa it has illegally gained a tenuous foothold in Libya, where its followers are hunted down by the police. For a while its criticism of Abdel Nasser's personal rule, his cult of per-sonality (*fardi*) which runs contrary to the popular (*shaabi*) regime promised by the Baathists seemed to have some effect, until Michel Aflaq's followers started to flounder in their own contradic-tions and intraparty strifes.

Nonetheless, to assume that only one nationalism moves the Arab world, that Abdel Nasser has a monopoly on Arab national-ism, would be in flagrant contradiction to reality. In the previous pages the elements of Arab unity and their practical realization in politics were enumerated. These components of unity were origi-nally created by Islam, or were at least strongly influenced by re-ligious factors. But still to be answered is the question: To what degree do these religious elements still determine the cultural and political development of the Arabs? If the Western world were described and its motivating forces analyzed by theologians, the elements of Christian unity would acquire special relief. A student of Romance languages would stress the signs of Latin cultural unity between Rumania in the east, the Italian and Iberian Peninsulas, France and the southern part of the western hemisphere; a Slav linguist would, in a similar vein, point out traces of common cul-ture from the Adriatic to Vladivostok. A historian of law might find a predominance of Roman law from Vietnam and Ceylon to Louisiana. But are such indications of unity relevant in modern history? Could there be created a common Christian front against heretics and infidels? Or is there any solidarity between the Latin nations? Not even the "Latin sisters," France and Italy, have shown particular bilateral closeness in the last hundred years.

4. Arab Dissensions

A. Secularism—A Centrifugal Force

Nationalism is not immutable; it changes. In the Arab countries it was originally closely linked to Pan-Islamism. The first declaration of a Pan-Arab national program at government level took place at the Islamic Congress in Jerusalem in 1931. In the years between the two world wars local nationalism prevailed. Now Pan-Arab nationalism is in ascendancy, or at least Arab leaders pay lip service to Pan-Arabism while at the same time they act as particularist nationalists. Pan-Arab unity is a myth, a strong myth, which may take concrete political shape in the creation of a single Arab state; but there exists no historical imperative that this must really happen. Many Arabs believe that Arab unity is predetermined, but history has shown as much Arab disunity as Arab unity in politics.

Nationalism's changing character has been pointed out in a recent book on Germany:

As nationalism assumed a mass character, it obviously lost its earlier idealistic complexion and became freighted with economic and social grievances. It tended to lose universal humanitarian aims and acquire a regional rootedness. It was more and more concerned with local autonomy and even national independence, which explains the decline of Pan-Slavism toward the end of the nineteenth century. This grass-roots nationalism ran counter to the centralism which had been the cornerstone of state power since the development of monarchical authority had undermined the local autonomy of the great feudal landowners. Bismarck recognized that nationalism in the West was a unifying factor but that to the East it was a divisive and revolutionary force which might undermine the public order established for centuries.[1]

The two sides of nationalism, its unifying and its divisive force, are active at the same time in the Arab world. While Pan-Arab nationalism agitates with enormous vocal strength, the separate Arab states consolidate themselves. Even in Jordan since 1960 this writer discovered the very first signs of a budding local patriotism in the Palestinians who constitute two-thirds of the population. Inside the borders of the Arab states, new loyalties are generated, new communities of interests are born, "parochial" thinking embraces the population; the "normativity of the factual" asserts itself. This may be deplored from the point of view of Pan-Arab nationalism, but the existence of the trend cannot be denied. Many politicians who proclaim their faith in Pan-Arab unity prefer, upon coming into power, to be big fish in a small pond rather than small fish in a big one. The Syrian experience has spoiled the taste of many Arab leaders for Arab political unity. The Arabs just recently have begun to emerge from the pre-political stage in which the solidarity of family, tribe, and religious group prevails over national unitarian thinking. In which mold the growing national feeling will flow, whether local, regional, or Pan-Arab nationalism, or a combination of these different forms, will gain the final victory, remains to be seen.

The most important integrating factor in the Arab world is still Islam, which impresses its seal on the whole of Arab civilization. But Islam in itself is a divided house. The schism between Sunnites and Shiites goes back to the earliest times of Muslim history. As can be observed in Iraq, the split has wide-reaching consequences in social life and politics. The main resistance against

Pan-Arab nationalism in Iraq comes from the Shiite side. Muhammad Hadid ventures the opinion: "The Sunnites are all for Abdel Nasser; the Christians and other minorities, especially the Shiites, would be against a union with Egypt."[2] The cleavage between Shiites and Sunnites is less clear in Syria and Lebanon. In Lebanon most of the Shiite leaders sided with the pro-Nasser faction in the civil war of 1958.

Heterodox practices, Maraboutism, and sects as well as old heresies like the Kharijite "deviation" and the Druse faith, which can be considered a separate religion, impair the unity of the Arab world. And then there are the non-Muslim groups. In the western Arab countries there still live several hundred thousand Jews— the exact number is hard to establish after the latest exodus from Morocco and Algeria. The Christians in the Maghreb are all immigrants from Europe. In Egypt, Jordan, Syria, and Iraq autochthonous Christians form important minority groups, and Lebanon is the only state in Asia, except the Philippines, with a Christian majority. The Christians in the Middle East have adopted Western technology with greater ease than have the Muslims. A traveler in the eastern Arab countries will meet mostly Christians as hotel and restaurant proprietors and employees. European-type shops and "American" supermarkets are more often than not run by Christians, as are taxis, garages, and other shops where gadgets and machinery are for sale. The Christians act as interpreters between the Muslim and the Western worlds and often form a sort of lubricating stratum. The Christians who support Pan-Arab nationalism in theory and practice can easily be counted. Most of them are members of the Arab intelligentsia. The vast majority of the rank and file, however, resists Pan-Arabism. They are afraid of being submerged again by the Muslim masses. The *millet* system has institutionalized religious separatism and created little fortresses of religious resistance against all "pan" movements. Pan-Arabists of all brands, therefore, attack these strongholds of parochialism as being against the principles of a modern state—which of course is true. But even Israel has not abolished the *millet* system inherited from the Ottoman Empire, which borrowed it from the Arab Empires preceding it. As explained, under this system all matters of personal status—marriage, divorce, burial, and some aspects of inheritance—are subject to the exclusive jurisdiction of religious courts.

Secularism tends to abolish the religious barriers between different Islamic groups and between the various religions. But at the same time it weakens the elements of unity in the Arab world. The energies freed by the removal of the traditional walls between the bulwarks of religious separatism are not *ipso facto* flowing into the broad channel of Pan-Arab nationalism, but tend to concentrate on the preservation of existing states. Maintaining the status quo seems to provide a certain guarantee against the uncertainties of the future.

Arab writers discuss how far secularization has already progressed. Sati al-Husri[3] goes so far as to claim that nationalism is a strictly secular which has nothing to do with religion. On the other hand, Zeine N. Zeine believes that nationalism is still dominated by religion: "The exponents of secular nationalism are still confined to a small class. Religion continues to be a dominating factor."[4] He asserts that the socialization of Arab nationalism "is the only way at present in which secularism can invade the fortress of Islam. . . . Advocates of secular, socialized Arab nationalism base their concept of nationalism on the 'community (the *umma*) feeling' of the Arabs and their 'natural cohesion' as Arabs."

Many more examples could be cited for one or the other point of view. The differences of opinion partly stem from secularism's unequal progress; we still find in the Arab world a theocracy side by side with an almost totally secularized state like Tunisia, where President Bourguiba even attempts to eliminate the unproductive fasting during the month of Ramadan. But even where secularization of Muslim society has reached a point comparable to the secularization of Western society, Islam still remains a dominating cultural factor. In Turkey non-Muslims, or converts like the Dönme, Muslims for many generations, are pointed out as something different, separate, and somehow not completely belonging to Turkish, basically Muslim, society. Islam, even where it does not determine the actions of men, is still the main topic in intellectual discussions, especially when East opposes West. That Islam still permeates Arab civilization becomes especially evident where Pan-Arabism holds sway; it has already been mentioned that the term *umma* has been transformed from meaning the "community of believers" to the "community of the nation." But also other terms connected with unity, *tawhid* (asserting oneness) and *ittihad* (union) are loaded with religious overtones.

In daily life Islamic rules are followed less and less. The most conspicuous outward symbol is, of course, the change in dress. Modern Arabs are ashamed of the traditional costumes; in Syria, when it was part of the United Arab Republic, taking pictures of farmers in oriental dress was forbidden, and the ban enforced by police—at least in Aleppo. Modern technology is responsible for the change in clothes. Any man invites a fatal accident working near a transmission belt or riding a motorcycle in a flowing dress. And how can a man pray five times a day—kneel and bow his head to the earth—in a Western hat, a tight jacket, and creased trousers?

The largest breach in the Islamic wall encircling Arab society has been broken by the elimination of most of the Koranic law. Except on the Arabian Peninsula, Islamic law has been reduced to a small residual part in a system which becomes more and more complex—as complex as the legal structure of the Western states. The *sharia* was God's law. To abolish it means doing without the rules set by God through his Prophet. The close-knit system organized by Muhammad is torn to pieces. Out of the all-embracing edifice of the Koran, an entire section has been torn out and thrown on the garbage heap of history.

Western law, of Roman and Germanic origin, has supplanted Islamic law. Constitutions provide for a division of powers, where there was once concentration in the hands of a caliph-sultan. Penal law follows European lines. Commercial law permits the lending of money at interest, and provides contractual guarantees; until recently a man's word was sufficient contract, and any other way of doing business was suspect. The law on personal status, dealing with birth and death, marriage and divorce, holds out longest against the onslaught of Western thinking. In Tunisia the Koranic law of persons has been eliminated, and Egypt has come close to abolishing the residue of *sharia* law.

The adoption of Western laws indicates a far-reaching cultural change. Not since the Holy Roman Empire of the German nation introduced and enforced Roman law in Germany at the end of the fifteenth century has there been such a far-reaching reception of foreign law. The Arabs in some cases have made original adaptations of the European law to their special conditions. But nevertheless this reception of alien laws brings a complete break with the past; the very foundations of social life are changed. Turkey's introduction of European law has been well publicized. The same process in the Arab countries is not less of an upheaval. No revolution could have achieved so much change in so short a time as has the reception of Western law. Law becomes separated from religion, and religion loses its normative power; its rules are not enforced by secular means. Religion becomes a set of unenforceable, non-obligatory ethical precepts, the disregard of which can only be punished in the other world. Religion is pushed from the core to the periphery of human thought and action; de-actualized, it changes its character. The following of external ritual practices becomes incidental: a non-believer may take part in the Friday prayer at the mosque, a believer may refrain from an outward testament toward his creed. In the process of secularization Islam is not initially consumed, it does not disappear completely but is transformed into a religion without God, like nationalism or communism (which may themselves be transformed from a political faith into mere modes of behavior and feeling).

Religion ceases to be the only motivating force. Its field of magnetism reduced, Western technology, Western habits, and Western law undermine its foundations. Western civilization is essentially a secularized civilization. Even history, as felt and understood by Arabs, is changing. The self-interpretation of the Arabs—mostly romantic until now—is more and more influenced by Western writers and Western ideologies. The writing of history is a powerful agent in creating a national consciousness. The realm of myth, legend, and genealogy will be left behind. By analyzing history, man and society acquire a past and sink roots into the fertile soil of reality. Archeology and history, however, reveal a pre-Islamic past as rich in many ways as the Islamic heritage. Whatever Pan-Arab nationalists may theorize, this pre-Islamic sphere is essentially non-Arab. Local nationalists in Algeria, in Egypt, in Lebanon, in Iraq all want to trace the ancestry of their nation to the oldest known stratum, just as the Turks have appropriated a Hittite and Sumerian heritage for their modern national state. Vertically, the elements of Arab unity are penetrated by historical research, which reaches down into pre-Islamic layers. Objective historical analysis tends to weaken the myth of Arab unity. Western history, with the assimilation of Western civilization, becomes also Arab history. The common past, history, is an abstraction with little reality to individuals or to the smallest social groups like family or *millet*; a Shiite will hardly accept "his" history as identical with a Sunnite's.[5]

Of all elements of Arab unity language remains the strongest. Its importance as an integrating factor in the Arab world is stressed by every writer, every politician. A common language may not necessarily form the basis for a nation. French, Italian, Spanish, Portuguese, English are spoken by more than one nation. Linguistic unity in the Arab countries is stronger now than it was fifty years ago. The modern means of communication have re-established contacts broken off in the "dark ages" of Arab history, the disintegration since the fall of the Abbassids and the hibernation under Ottoman rule. Jacques Berque even speaks of a "linguistic renaissance which permits the circulation of sentiments of unity from the Atlantic Ocean to the Persian Gulf."[6] But he also points out how dialects assert themselves in speech and literature.[7] This appears enormously important because language for the Arab is not a means to describe reality, it is a reality itself, separate from the world of things. Using dialect, a writer digs deeper into the facts of daily life, describes better the sorrows and expectations of the people, but he is separated from the upper reaches of soaring ideas and dreams. In a different way, the Arab technician withdraws from the classical language. Probably his technical training has been in French or English or Italian; for technical explanations he may either use the foreign language, or lard his Arabic with borrowed words, which flow more easily over his tongue than the complicated derivations from ancient Arabic roots. Dialects and borrowings do not destroy the language, but they add new dimensions which increase the distance of modern usage from the Koranic idiom. A new language is emerging in newspapers and literature, simplified in its structure, but more adaptable to the needs of a technological civilization—a secularized Arabic. As the Greek language in Hellenistic times transformed Oriental modes of thinking and speaking, so European languages today influence not only the Arab language but also the train of ideas.

B. Local Nationalism

Observing Egypt, one could assume that Pan-Arab nationalism is the final stage of development. In the Asian Arab countries Pan-Arab nationalism has its ups and downs but holds large parts of the population in its grip. The idea that Arab national feeling could flow not into one but into several different molds is utterly despicable to Pan-Arab nationalists. An Arab nationalist like Malek Bennabi, on the other hand, declares: "The formulas like Pan-Arabism and Pan-Islamism are obsolete now."[8] However, unity seems no closer to realization than it was, say, in 1956. Particularism, inherent in the European conception of "the nation," actually prevails over Pan-Arab nationalism. After the revolution of July 14, 1958, in Baghdad, many observers believed that unity was only one step away. Syria had already joined Egypt in the United Arab Republic, and Yemen was drawn into the United Arab States, a confederation of sovereign states which evolved toward a federation with unified foreign and military policies. Saudi Arabia concluded a defense agreement with Egypt, the strongest of the Arab states. General Kassem and most of his followers at one time or another had voiced their sympathy for Arab unity. Far-reaching agreements for co-operation in the fields of economy, education, and defense were concluded between Baghdad and the United Arab Republic. In Lebanon, where the pro-Nasser forces openly rebelled against the regime of President Chamoun, it was touch and go for a while as to who would win the struggle. Suddenly the Pan-Arab drive for unity and power collapsed like a punctured balloon.

Pan-Arabism got its second wind in the spring of 1963, when Egypt, Syria, and Iraq decided to form a union. The project only lived a few weeks. Pan-Arab nationalists who tend to ascribe every set-back to foreign intervention blame the American landing in Lebanon in 1958 for their lack of success. Indeed the Arabs as far east as Baghdad and Kuwait were extraordinarily impressed by the superior technical equipment the American armed forces brought with them. Abdel Nasser's claim to victory over the united Israeli, French, and British forces in 1956 paled before American power evidenced for all eyes. And Khrushchev's bluff was called most clearly. While the Soviet dictator had threatened to use rockets and atom bombs to help defeat colonialist aggression, no action followed in this case. The Arabs are sensitive to all the political winds which flow from East or West over the deserts; they understood the message. But American forces did not intervene in Arab affairs; they guaranteed to a small state its right to separate existence, according to a principle also upheld by the United Nations. This right in former times could only be safeguarded by military might and skillful diplomacy. However muddled the actions and declarations of the United Nations in the case of Lebanon may have been, the intent finally was made clear: sovereign states shall not be subjugated against their will.

This manifestation of the intents of the United Nations followed shortly after a reversal of policy by the Soviet Union. At first, Moscow and the Communist parties had supported Pan-Arab nationalism, mainly for its nuisance value toward the West, forcing Britain to give up colonial positions in the Middle East and promoting bias against the West in Arab countries. When Syria turned toward Egypt to form the United Arab Republic, the Communist party was the only political party there which refused to dissolve itself on Abdel Nasser's bidding. In Syria and Iraq the Communists turned openly against Arab unity, and the united Syro-Lebanese party was split into independent entities, according to the principle of separate parties for separate countries.[9] Everywhere, however, nationalism has proved stronger even than Marxist internationalism where this is not enforced by Russian tanks.

In Iraq the age-old antagonism between the Land-of-two-Rivers and the Nile Valley has prevailed over the idea of Arab unity. Abdul Karim Kassem in a personal talk with the author in December, 1958, stressed his belief in Arab unity. However, he did not use the word "*umma*," nation, but employed the less substantial "*watan*," fatherland, when speaking of the Arab world. Kassem did not want to be drawn into a new Arab empire in which Baghdad would contribute its oil assets but would revert to a dusty outpost, as it was under Ottoman rule. Since his violent death, new proclamations of the will to establish Arab unity have been heard, coming first from the Baathist, then from Aref.

Syria has lost its self-confidence as a nation. Damascus, once the capital of an Arab empire, later the most important center of Ottoman administration in Asian Arabia, and one of the birthplaces of modern Arab nationalism, swings like a pendulum first toward Iraq, then toward Egypt. For more than ten years, it has waged countless economic "wars" against Lebanon and Jordan, closing the borders, re-opening the borders, restricting imports, demanding higher transit fees from trucks and pipelines, showing discontent with itself and everybody else. Military dictators come and go, and agreement on a steady course cannot be reached. Impressive economic progress was made, however, until 1957, and education has spread rapidly to all classes of the population. Nowhere has the old social structure been destroyed to such a degree as in Syria by the invasion of Western civilization. Bedouin restlessness afflicts nomads and settlers alike and combines nefariously with the rootlessness of city masses. As a nucleus of national consciousness, Syria has lost its former influence.

Kuwait, Saudi Arabia, and Jordan have reached only the first stages of national feeling. Dynasties and tribal leaders still dominate politics, based on pre-national loyalties and tradition-bound rule. Yemen is torn by civil war. Sudan, divided into "white" (Arab) and "black" (Negro), fights hard for national integration. The Muslims are split into religio-political sects, the pagan Negroes into tribes with different cultures, different tongues. Sudan has resisted absorption into Egypt under whose hegemony it lived for centuries, while the "black" south was a traditional hunting ground for slaves.

Lebanon is the spectrum of all the forces at work in the Arab world. There exists hardly a political or religious tendency which is not represented in Lebanon. Culturally it looks toward the West, toward Paris first, toward the United States increasingly in recent times. Hundreds of thousands of Lebanese, a majority of them Christians, work in foreign countries, some even in Iceland, send home their checks, and return with new ideas to their mountain villages. They have terraced their rocky, barren mountains up to six thousand feet and have developed one of the most intensive agricultures in the world. Lebanese fruit does not find its equal in the Middle East or in America; but lack of standards and a facile outlet in the Arab countries, where there is little competition, have impaired exports to the West. The Lebanese are proud of their achievements; "the pyramids of the Egyptians are a hundred meters high, ours mount two thousand meters toward heaven," lyrically exclaims the Lebanese Charles Corm in his book, *La Montagne inspirée*, as he looks at the terraced mountains of his fatherland.[10] But even more than pride, commercial shrewdness determines Lebanese behavior.

Lebanon was overrun by conquerors countless times in history; many of whom left their marks on the rocks near Nahr al-Kalb. In Ottoman times Lebanon acquired a certain degree of feudal autonomy when Christians and Druses collaborated, and this co-operation still is one of the bases of the sovereign state. The National Covenant, an unwritten agreement, concluded by Riad as-Solh for the Sunnite Muslims and Beshara al-Khuri for the Maronite Christians, after twenty years still retains validity as the foundation for peaceful political co-operation of the two largest denominations. Even though infringed often in recent times, politicians always fall back on this act of statesmanship.

In the turbulent times of 1956 to 1958, when pro-Nasser forces launched two minor and one major attempt to grasp power by force in Lebanon, the political split ran through the entire population, whatever their religious belief. The Maronite Patriarch, Meouchi, for personal reasons stood against the Maronite President of the Republic, Camille Chamoun, while the Maronite commander in chief of the armed forces, and later President, Fuad Shehab, tried from the sidelines to separate the litigants. The Druse community was split right through the middle, one faction, led by Kamal Jumblat, fighting against Chamoun, the other, led by Emir Majid Arslan, with him. The vast majority of the Sunnites were up in arms against the government headed by the Sunnite Prime Minister Sami as-Solh, and most of the Shiite feudal lords sided with the Sunnite majority group. Chamoun found his toughest allies in the Popular (or National) Socialist party (former

Syrian People's party) which fights with every means for a Greater Syria, and in the Kataeb, the phalanx of Pierre Gemayel, chiefly a Maronite Christian militant party. The struggle ended in a compromise with regard to the distribution of political offices and patronage (it could hardly be expected differently in Lebanon) but left the independence of the state intact. When the chips were down, Lebanese nationalism clearly prevailed over Pan-Arab nationalism, and the Sunnite leaders who had shown the greatest admiration for Abdel Nasser had to accept this nationalism as a fact. Local nationalists, who like to vaunt their descent from the ancient Phoenicians, may paint a fanciful picture of history, but in 1958 they proved their readiness to fight, and fight successfully, for independent Lebanon.

Even more than Damascus, Beirut can claim to be the birthplace of Arab nationalism. It was here that the young Ibrahim al-Yaziji recited in 1868, before the Syrian Learned Society, his famous hymn, beginning:

> Arise, O Arabs, from sleep awake!
> Knee-deep we're sunk in misery's lake . . .

It was in Beirut at the first two modern universities of the Middle East that young Arab intellectuals were brought into contact with the ideas of the American and French revolutions. Christians participated, or took the lead, in the developing nationalist movement directed against Ottoman misrule and Young Turk centralism. At first this movement was a general feeling diffuse in intellectual circles rather than an organization. In the Lebanese mountains the desire for autonomy or independence had been kept alive under Fahreddin al-Maani and Beshir II Shehab, and it found a first fulfilment when a guarantee for local autonomy was extracted from the Sultan by a French expeditionary force. The mountains along the Mediterranean coast have always provided persecuted minorities with a sanctuary. The Lebanese Republic is still composed of minorities, no single group forming a majority. The minorities tend to organize themselves along religious lines, and this is sanctioned by the constitution. Their principal interest is to resist being submerged again in an empire, and at the same time to keep the doors open to the rest of the Arab world. This has been achieved up to now. Local nationalism has resisted autocratic Pan-Arab nationalism successfully.

Egypt, of course, economically and militarily the strongest of the Arab countries, developed before any other Arab region a dynastic nationalism under Muhammad Ali, the Albanian mercenary leader who took power in the wake of Napoleon's Egyptian campaign. He started the first program of industrialization, which petered out after his death. None of his projects either asked for, or found, large scale popular support. Modern nationalism was restricted to the Egyptian state—a local nationalism par excellence until recent times. Ancient history and the Pharaohs were glorified, and in general Egyptians did not venture far from the Nile Valley. Nationalism found its roots in history many thousand years before the Arab and Islamic conquest. The ruling dynasty and the leading families looked to Europe. The Khedive Ismail proclaimed, after the Suez Canal had increased Egyptian contacts with the Western world: "Egypt is part of Europe now." Muhammad Abduh, Pan-Islamist and religious reformer, exclaimed: "Every Egyptian ought to love his native country." And Saad Zaghlul, founder of the first nationalist mass party, the Wafd, opined: "Our problem is an Egyptian problem and not an Arab problem." He rejected Pan-Arabism violently: "If you add one zero to another zero, then you add another zero, what will be the sum?"[11]

Egypt for a long time had been a separate entity in the Ottoman Empire. It is isolated by deserts from its neighbors to the east and to the west. Descent from one of the oldest civilizations of the world is obvious to every Egyptian, whose eyes cannot avoid seeing pyramids and other signs of a splendid past. Not until the 1930's did a real Egyptian interest awake in the Pan-Arab movement. An extremely cool reception was given even in Egypt to the "Qudsi Plan" in 1951, named after its proponent, Nazim al-Qudsi, at that time Prime Minister of Syria and in 1962 President of the Syrian

Republic, who advocated Arab unification in the form of a confederation, a federation, or a complete union. After World War II Egypt started to play a leading role in the League of Arab States, and since the advent of Abdel Nasser in 1952 Cairo has developed its own brand of Pan-Arab nationalism. Its violent methods created resistance where originally sympathy for the revolution's aims prevailed. Abdel Nasser is deeply engaged in organizing Arab socialism in his country, his army is engaged in the war in Yemen, and his propaganda for Arab unity has not ceased.

The Maghreb, or the Arab West, has never been as thrilled by the Pan-Arab ideal as has the Arab East. Historically it lies on an important north-south axis of cultural diffusion, which is as decisive as the Islamic east-west axis. European influence has always been felt strongly in North Africa. The colonial rule to which it was subjected brought in European settlers and changed the social, economic, and political structure of the countries.

Libya now swims on a wave of prosperity brought by the discovery of oil. This "constitutional theocracy" is little integrated as a nation. Appeals from Egypt based on Pan-Arab nationalism and calls from the west for a Maghreb Federation draw the city-dwellers in different directions, while the majority, nomads of the desert, still mainly pursue their tribal interests. Tunisia, under Habib Bourguiba's autocratic rule, was for many years the great antagonist of Abdel Nasser's Egypt, especially because the conflict between the two *zaïms* has been so highly personalized. Even under French rule Tunisia remained a separate if non-sovereign state, kept its special traditions and its own administration. If there were strong leanings toward Pan-Arab nationalism, they could not show under the present regime.

Algeria's National Liberation Front has accepted aid from Egypt as it has from other countries. Its leaders moved, however, from Cairo to Tunis, not only to be nearer the scene of the war for liberation, but also to acquire more freedom of maneuver. The meetings of the highest organ of the revolution, the Council of the Revolution, were often held in Tripoli to be away from any strong man's intervention. Independence brought Algerian leaders nearer to Abdel Nasser. "Islamic socialism" as applied in Egypt and Algeria shows many common features. No pact of unity has been concluded between the two countries, although the collaboration between Abdel Nasser and Ben Bella is very close.

Morocco can claim to be the oldest of all modern Arab states. Only from 1912 to 1956 was it temporarily a French and Spanish protectorate. That Morocco would ever give up its separate personality and dissolve itself in a centralized Arab state seems highly unlikely, whatever the proclamations of political leaders for purposes of internal politics may be.

The main struggle in the Arab world takes place between Gamal Abdel Nasser and his adherents on one side and the local nationalists in a dozen Arab countries on the other side. The centripetal forces in the Arab world are still too weak to form one united Arab state. More could have been accomplished if Egypt's energies had been channeled toward bringing about a federation, instead of attempting creation of a centralized state. Neither Egypt, nor anyone else, seems to command the necessary forces to build, administratively and politically, an Arab state reaching from the Atlantic Ocean to the Persian Gulf. Economically the whole area suffers from an unsurmounted weakness: all Islamic countries, where Muslims are a majority or a strong minority, belong to the so-called underdeveloped area, the region which has not yet fully developed its material and human resources and lacks the production facilities common to the Western world. Getting rid of colonialism remains only a first step; the next is to overcome the special social and economic conditions which unwittingly invite colonial aspirations from without.

C. Regional Nationalism

While the battle between Nasserists and local nationalists weaves back and forth, a third rival gets into the fray: regional nationalism. The idea, to offest the dispersal of Arab forces and the Balkanization of the Arab world by uniting several states into regional groups, is not new; it grew from two sources: the dynastic aspirations of the Hashemites and from economic interaction. There exist four geologically well-defined regions in the Arab world: (1) the Fertile Crescent with Iraq, Syria, Jordan, Lebanon —and, according to the Arabs, the part of Palestine which has become Israel; (2) the Arabian Peninsula with Yemen, Saudi Arabia, and Kuwait, together with the dependent principalities along the coast from Aden to the Persian Gulf; (3) the Nile Valley with Egypt and Sudan; and (4) the Maghreb with Libya, Tunisia, Algeria, Morocco, and Mauritania. Each of these regions in the course of history has developed similarities and common interests, distinct from all the other parts of the Arab world.

The Arabs of the Fertile Crescent feel closely linked together by historical bounds, but the western part—Syria, Lebanon, and Palestine—has been a battle-ground between the rulers of Mesopotamia and the Nile Valley since times immemorial. After World War I the Hashemites, helped on the thrones of Baghdad and Amman by the British, tried to unite the area under their own scepters. Nuri as-Said, head of thirteen governments in Iraq and dominating many more behind the scenes, submitted a Fertile Crescent Plan in his Blue Book of 1943. Emir (later King) Abdullah of Jordan worked for a similar union, partly at cross-purposes with his relatives on the throne in Baghdad. Syria's *hizb al-shaab,* the most influential party after World War II, whose leaders came again to power after the secession from the United Arab Republic, expressed a special interest in the Fertile Crescent idea. In part, this was because Aleppo, the homebase of the People's party, is traditionally the principal station on the way from the Mediterranean Sea or from Turkey to Mosul and Baghdad and even farther east. A fourth force also working toward unification of the countries in the Fertile Crescent is the Popular (or National) Socialist party, now banned in all the countries of the Arab East. The Popular

Socialist party was founded by a Christian, Antun Saadeh, who saw himself as the founder of a Greater Syria. Greater Syria would comprise more or less the same lands as the Fertile Crescent; the main difference would be that it would get Damascus as a center, instead of Baghdad, or, as some Palestinians might wish, Jerusalem. The party used terror as a means of action. And terror was met by equivalent repression: Antun Saadeh fell before a Lebanese firing squad. The party fought in the forefront against the adherents of Gamal Abdel Nasser in the Lebanese civil war of 1958. It was the main target of Abdul Hamid Sarraj's persecution in Syria. On New Year's Eve, 1961, the party attempted a *Putsch* in Lebanon which failed. Organized like an army, the party prefers "direct" action to political maneuvering—and pays the price for this attitude. Its socialism has little resemblance to Western socialism; the combination of nationalism with socialism here again seems to create a fateful mixture of highly explosive potency.

Abdul Karim Kassem had taken up the idea of the Fertile Crescent; how seriously remains a mystery. From time to time he uttered ambiguous words to the effect that a Fertile Crescent federation or union should be organized. But the declamations were never followed by any visible action. When the Syrian Prime Minister, Bashir al-Azmah, on June 6, 1962, called for a "federal union" between Syria, Egypt, and Iraq, Abdul Karim Kassem proclaimed at a university graduation ceremony in Baghdad on June 15: "The Iraqi flag will fly in Iraq and the Syrian flag will fly in Syria. But the frontiers between us will disappear, for we are one people and one country."[12] Kassem, whose regime was characterized as "authoritarian anarchy," could never muster the necessary dynamism to form a Fertile Crescent community.

The unity of the Arabian Peninsula was on the mind of King Abdul Aziz ibn Saud; but it remained a vision never realized. Ibn Saud backed away from a conquest of Yemen, and in the later years of his life remained peacefully inside his oil-rich domains. His sons, King Saud and Emir Faisal, could hardly mobilize the strength to accomplish a union. None of the monarchs could unify the Arabian Peninsula. The last of the Hashemite rulers, King Hussein of Jordan, for many years has fought a brave battle for his and his country's survival, and this absorbs all his resources.

The unity of the Nile Valley seemed close to realization when Sudan gained its independence in January, 1956. The party which then took power had previously advocated union with Egypt, but when it held the reins of government in its hands, local nationalism and self-interest asserted themselves, and Sudan has remained a separate, sovereign state. *Al-bilad as-sudan,* the Land of the Blacks, strives hard to keep its Arabized Muslims and its pagan Negro parts together. Union with Egypt might lead to an irreparable schism, the peoples of the southern regions asserting their "African personality" which is completely different from the Arab one.

The most concrete and serious attempts at regional unification have been made in North Africa. The Berber substratum, increasing in strength from east to west, and the past common overlordship by the French, confer a special character on the Maghreb. The Maghreb without any doubt comprises Morocco, Algeria, and Tunisia; Libya, separated from its neighboring states by deserts and subdivided by the Sahara which reaches to the coast, remains contested territory between the Nile Valley and the Maghreb. The Maghreb leaders include it in their sphere, but strong counter-influences emanate from Cairo.

A Maghreb Federation can only be realized when North Africa has reached a certain political stability. It was first agreed upon in a conference on April 28-30, 1958, by the Istiqlal party of Morocco, the National Liberation Front of Algeria (FLN), and the Neodestour party of Tunisia, all three of which had a political monopoly or near-monopoly in their areas. In the years since this agreement of Tangiers, the Istiqlal has split into the "old" Istiqlal and the Union of Popular Forces and furthermore received competition in new parties, mainly the Haraka Chaabia, Ahmed Reda Guedira's parties, and the Communists. The Algerian FLN suffers from acute growing pains and a power struggle between its leaders. And Habib Bourguiba, as usual, would like everything to go according to his ideas. To lift the question from the party level to the level of binding governmental decisions would call for the immediate solution of two pressing problems: First, the question of leadership and the methods of co-operation in the Federation and second, the question of the borders between the member states. Border conflicts led to the small-scale war between Algeria and Morocco in October, 1963. Furthermore, the distribution of the riches of the Sahara would have to be agreed upon. To bring secular and socialist Algeria under one hat with the constitutional monarchy in Morocco and the "enlightened dictatorship" in Tunisia is not an easy accomplishment. Reason prevailing, a Maghreb Federation could be created to the mutual benefit of all North Africa.

The trend toward regional integration today appears much weaker than the warring local and Pan-Arab nationalisms which exert a strong emotional appeal. In the long run, geographical proximity, common economic interests, and the socio-political pressures to overcome exaggerated pluralism might work toward regional co-operation, if not unification. Since nothing is fixed, everything is fluid in the Arab world, predictions have to be avoided. What seems in the cards one day has vanished when the next sun rises; what appears impossible at present may be realized tomorrow.

D. *Arab Imperialism*

Arab nationalists tend to enlarge cartographically the borders of the lands where Arabs live. A map published by L'Association Internationale des Amis du Monde Arabe (Lausanne-Munich), widely used in publications emanating from Cairo, shows the frontiers of the Arab world reaching as far east as the Zagros mountains in Iran (Persia), north to the Taurus mountains in Turkey; in the south it includes Somalia and the sovereign states of Chad,

Niger, Mali (all three predominately populated by non-Arab Muslims), and of course, Mauritania. This map corresponds to the dream which Pan-Arab nationalists have of their future unified Arab state.

The extensive interpretation of borders corresponds to the Islamic principle that no part of the Domain of Islam (dar al-Islam) can be given up legally by a Muslim. In this case again the Muslim creed lies at the basis of Arab nationalist claims. In Syria all maps show the former Sandshak of Alexandrette (Hatay) as Syrian territory. During Syria's membership in the United Arab Republic this claim was renewed with increasing force. Hardly anybody could claim in good faith that an Arab majority exists today in the region ceded to Turkey immediately before World War II. But many Arab nationalists go further and demand the extension of Arab rule as far north as the Taurus mountains, including the plains of Adana, Tarsus, and Mersin. It is true that parts of the population in Southern Turkey understand or speak Arabic. The linguistic frontiers are never cleanly drawn, and Turks and Arabs have lived side by side in this area for centuries, but any claim to tear away Adana, or even Iskenderun, from Turkey would meet with the concerted opposition of the Turkish nation—and its army.

Cyprus is claimed by the founder of the Popular Socialist party (Greater Syria party) as Arab land; Antun Saadeh called it "the star before the Fertile Crescent." The Muslim population, however racially mixed it may be, feels itself Turkish, not Arab. The only close-knit Arab community—about 1 per cent of the total population, compared to about 18 per cent Turks—are Maronites from Lebanon, part of whom have been settled on the Copper Isle since the Middle Ages. The Lebanese interceded for them after Cyprus gained its independence and won political representation for the Maronites. They received it, not at the expense of Muslim Turks, but offered by the Christian Greeks. When Archbishop Makarios first visited Egypt, Anwar as-Sadat, one of the leaders of

Abdel Nasser's regime, publicly recognized the Cypriot Greeks' demand for self-determination, but let it be known that Arabs also have a special interest in Cyprus.

In 1961, Iraq's claim to Kuwait troubled the diplomatic waters. Iraq refrained from taking military action against the little principality with its fabulous riches. Abdul Karim Kassem's claim was based on the fact that Kuwait, like Iraq, belonged once to the Ottoman Empire. But so did other Arab territories, including for example Yemen, which moreover did not participate in the uprising against the Turks in World War I. While Arabs demand those regions Arabs once settled, they do not think of granting independence to the Muslim Kurds, who under no title can be considered Arabs. Neither would Turkey or Iran be willing to grant independence to the Kurds. The Damascenes have never been completely reconciled to the existence of Jordan as a sovereign state. Countless times Jordan has been mentioned as the darkest corner of the former (Turkish) Vilayet of Damascus.

Similar problems crop up in North Africa. The frontiers of the oil-rich Sahara are contested by the border states. Habib Bourguiba let Tunisian troops attack in the Sahara under the smokescreen of the struggle for Bizerte. When they marched forward they found the Algerian rebel flag already planted near the place where Bourguiba wanted to establish the new border—and then the Tunisian troops were bombed by French planes and had to withdraw with heavy losses. The anti-colonialist slogans used in the conflict about Bizerte were so blinding that the incident in the desert was not even mentioned during the debate in the United Nations—or by France's allies.

Morocco claims more territory in North Africa than any other Arab state. Moroccans tend to take as self-evident that all the Spanish possessions on North African soil must revert to the Sherifian Kingdom. These Spanish domains are the enclave of Ifni and Rio de Oro (claimed also by Mauritania) on the Atlantic coast, five little isles in the Mediterranean—three, Islas Chafarinas, Peñon de Alhucemas, and Peñon de la Gomera, with all together about fifteen hundred inhabitants—and the two coastal towns of Ceuta and Melilla. Ceuta has belonged uninterruptedly to Portugal or Spain since 1415, and Melilla since 1497; only about 10 per cent of their populations are Muslims.

Morocco wants to extend its borders as far south as the Senegal River. It lays claim to the whole of Mauritania, an independent state, member of the United Nations. Furthermore, Morocco demands from the new Algerian government a settlement of its claims to certain territories in the Sahara which were administered as part of the Sahara departments by France, but where no borders have ever been clearly drawn. Twice in the first seven months of 1962 Morocco tried to establish a *fait accompli* in these territories by occupying border posts and desert wells. The first time, the Moroccans were pushed back by the French, the second by the Algerians. On July 5, 1962, Moroccans occupied the border post of Saf-Saf, while at the same time they let a delegation from Tindouf swear allegiance to King Hassan. In October, 1963, heavy fighting broke out along the Algerian-Moroccan border from Figuig in the north as far as the region of Tindouf in the south and especially near Hassi Beida and Tinjoub. Finally the mediation of the Organization of African Unity brought about an armistice. Morocco recognizes only the eighty miles of border from the Mediterranean coast to the Teniet-Sassi pass. The southern part of the border was drawn and re-drawn by the French, the last time in 1910, and recognized by Sultan Mohammed in 1928 as an administrative and fiscal demarcation line but not as a political frontier. In April, 1961, King Hassan II concluded a secret agreement with Ferhat Abbas, then head of the Provisional Government of the Algerian Republic (GPRA), in which the Algerians agreed that due to the arbitrary drawing of border lines by the French, territorial questions might arise which should be cleared up in talks between the sovereign states. Algeria at that time had not yet gained independence. A final solution of the conflict has not yet been reached, notwithstanding the hard work of the representatives of the Organization of African Unity (OAU). The organization's Charter of Addis Ababa recognizes the validity of the existing borders in Africa, although most of them were drawn by colonial powers. Moroccan claims to the vast desert areas are based mostly on former feudal allegiance of tribal leaders to the Sultan of Morocco, in other words on personal relationships of a feudal type. However, territorial rule has not been maintained by Moroccan sultans over the claimed territories in the southern desert for centuries. If history were a valid yardstick, Mauretania could demand control over Morocco, because the last great Arab-Berber empire (of the Almohads), which included present-day Morocco and Spain, emerged originally from Mauretania.

E. Arab Nationalism versus Israel

Many commentators on the Arab world see the state where Jewish nationalism—which took the form of Zionism—found its fulfilment as the cause, or at least a main factor, in the development of Arab nationalism.[13] However, it seems to this writer that none of the problems which assail the Arab world today have been created by the existence of Israel. Some issues have been set in sharper focus, and Arab nationalism may have developed in a different direction due to Israel. Arab nationalists see Israel as one of the ancient *millets,* the Jewish one, that has made itself independent and has annexed Islamic land; it has cut away a piece of the Domain of Islam and this no Muslim should tolerate. To do this Israel relied on the help of colonial and neo-colonialist powers —the British who proclaimed the Balfour Doctrine and permitted settlement of Jews in the Mandate Territory of Palestine, the Americans who financed to a great extent the Jewish project and gave support in the United Nations, the French who sent arms and volunteers. Envy of the people who have mastered Western technology and who profit from fully partaking in Western civilization plays a certain role. The old conception of the inviolable Dar al-Islam mixes with the hatred of colonialists and imperialists. The wars of 1948 and 1956 and many border skirmishes showed up the military weakness of the Arabs and their disunity. This again increases their desire to cling together, to form one mighty state that could deal with cheeky Israel. Israel thus has acted as a catalyst by which Arab nationalism inflames itself and finds its only unity of purpose, and it has pushed Arab nationalists in the direction of Pan-Arab unity and its most violent protagonist, Abdel Nasser, who promises to set up a counter-pole to Israel's military power. But the same nationalism which keeps the Eastern Arab countries in upheaval can be seen at work in North Africa, where Israel is of little concern to the population.

The Arabs assert that they are only fighting Zionism, that they do not want to exterminate the Jews. But none of the many Arab leaders this writer has spoken to showed any intention of putting up with the existence of Israel as a sovereign state. That Israel has been recognized by a vast majority of states, and that it has been accepted as a member of the United Nations, does not matter much to Arab nationalists; *sub specie aeternitatis* Israel has to disappear as a sovereign entity. How this should be accomplished nobody yet seems to know, but all steps taken thus far in the United Nations—for the implementation of the resolutions about the partition of Palestine and the return of refugees, and by the different Arab governments to create a Palestinian "government" or a Palestinian "army," should be considered only as steps toward the "final solution."

F. Nationalism and Communism

The tensions which make the Arab world tremble have not been created by communism; but Communists draw profit from the continuous unrest. Communism in the Middle East is not the subject of this book, but a few ideas about the problem may nevertheless be submitted. Communism acts on the two levels of inter-governmental relations and of party agitation. Khrushchev's decision to support bourgeois-nationalist, anti-colonialist groups whatever their attitude toward communism opened new vistas, first for Abdel Nasser, then for other Arab governments in their anti-Western politics. They could receive arms not granted by Western powers which wanted to preserve the status quo and peace in the Middle East. Older weapons, filtered from the arsenals now filled with Russian and Czech material, turned up in Oman and in Mauritania, and nobody could complain that these guns were Soviet-made. Economic and technical aid from Moscow balances Western financial support and gives some countries the intoxicating feeling of being independent in every field and able to play one power against the other to an Arab's own profit. The USSR gives generous diplomatic support in the United Nations, threatening alleged aggressors with rockets and atom bombs. As long as a government proves a certain nuisance value to the West, the Soviets are ready to underwrite the costs. But they believe, like other Communists, that nationalism or national-socialism are only transitory phenomena which prepare the way for the final victory of communism. To them, many an oriental state must seem to be administered by Oblomov and defended by the Good Soldier Svejk. Which opens marvellous expectancies for the Communists. . . .

Meanwhile Moscow offers the Arabs and other African and Asian countries an alternative to trading, bargaining, and dealing with Western Europe or the United States, the two immense production centers which, excepting Japan, alone provide the underdeveloped states with everything from foodstuff to machinery and arms. But, to their discomfort, Africans and Asians have discovered that Russians are white, too. Furthermore, their intellectual structure is built on the same foundations as those of the West, namely the Hebrew-Christian-Greek-Roman civilization, which after different transformations has produced the dominating technology.

Most Asians and Africans fail to see what basically divides the Soviets from the West: freedom, self-determination of the individual, human rights—values developed to a high degree in the West during the last two centuries. Seen from Asia and Africa, Russia and the West fit together like the two halves of a walnut shell. And there are as many "Ugly Russians" as there are "Ugly Americans" around. But Moscow, situated on the vast plains open to the east, lies nearer the threshold between the Western world and Asia and seems more accessible to many colored Orientals than do many Western capitals.

Chinese Communists today also compete with Soviet Communists in Africa and Asia. The ideological background of the power struggle between the two Communist colossi interests the emerging peoples less than the possibilities to extract aid from both of them. The Chinese play on the nationalist feelings of the Arabs even more than the Russians. Peiping's financial and diplomatic support, however, cannot equal Moscow's. Chinese advice led to some of the most spectacular failures of the Iraqi Communists in Kassem's time. The Iraqi Communists demanded that the land owned by the state, or expropriated in the course of land reform, be organized in state farms (*sovkhoses*) and not handed over to the land-hungry peasants. The loss of mass support was the inevitable consequence. Chinese Communist imperialism is seldom felt as a threat by the Arabs because the power basis of Mao Tsetung is so far away. And sometimes the farthest ally seems the best ally.

Communist techniques of command in economics and politics, which appear thoroughly Asian to Europeans and Americans, appeal to some of the new rulers in the Arab world. Statism has older models in the Arab world: Muhammad Ali's short-lived attempt to build up industries in Egypt may serve as an example. And the old "hydraulic societies" of the Nile Valley and of Mesopotamia are geared to close co-operation in the distribution of water and the use of land, under central command of village elders, feudal lords, or the government. Central command of the economy all too often transfers individual inefficiency, maladjustment to modern civilization, and lack of initiative from the more innocuous level of private enterprise to the authority-endowed level of the state and its bureaucracy.

Autocratic rule has been established in nearly all Islamic countries. The desire to overcome the pluralism of society by force, to eliminate the human variable, to avoid the possibility of becoming victim of a change, is all-pervading in authoritarian regimes. What method could better overcome the unpredictable than communism, which promises a planned miraculous leap into a glorious future? The belief in the analytical qualities of Marxism may be genuine or only a rationalization of an ambitious leader, but the Communist methods for the organization of the people are highly attractive to leaders in new-born states. Several governments try to apply some of the principles of Soviet organization in agrarian co-operatives or in workers' brigades. Moroccans seemed for a while especially impressed by the Chinese mobilization of manpower. We do not know whether information about failure after failure of organization and planning, in agriculture, in the backyard steel furnaces—which doom the Chinese to hunger and misery—has penetrated now to the enthusiastic supporters of Chinese methods in Rabat and Casablanca. The disillusionment might merge with the disappointment over Russia's sharp bargain which led to the admittance of Mauritania to the United Nations. Important parties have adopted the Communist organization plan: the Baath party, the Kurdish Democratic party in Iraq, the National Liberation Front in Algeria, and, to a lesser degree, the Neodestour party of Habib Bourguiba and the Union of Popular Forces in Morocco. None of these parties is a Communist party, all are nationalist organizations which use Communist methods, and they may, or may not, be pro-Soviet.

On the party level, communism agitates in partial or total illegality. Until 1963, the only Arab country where a Communist party was completely legal—but held on a very short leash—was Tunisia. In Morocco the party battled in the courts for legalization, but lost. In Iraq, since Kassem's fall, the Communists are hunted down by the police. In Lebanon the Communists are officially banned, but actually tolerated, and they publish two newspapers. Abdel Nasser never battled communism on an ideological basis. The Egyptian leader fought the Communists because they were against his Pan-Arabist plans. Abdel Nasser branded them as enemies of Arab unity—like the Zionists. The Communists' ideology and their subservience to Moscow, or to China, seem matters of secondary importance to the Arab *zaïms* . . . .

The Communists use many different approaches to the peoples of the Arab world. They cultivate minorities, infiltrate trade unions, play up to churches, and cater to *ulemas*. In the elections for the Greek-Orthodox Patriarchs of Jerusalem and of Antiochia (in Damascus) and for the Armenian-Orthodox Patriarch in Beirut, pro-Soviet candidates received each time about one-third of the vote. When Abdel Nasser prodded the sheikhs of al-Azhar to condemn communism, the *ulemas* of Baghdad—at the time of Kassem's rule—answered that they should not mix religion and politics. Intellectuals and politicians are invited to Moscow and the satellite capitals, flattered and honored and given status.

Islam may be, as some observers argue, a bulwark against communism, but so is the Catholic church. However, the only mass parties the Communists have been able to build up outside of the Soviet and Chinese orbit exist in France and Italy, and Cuba is a Catholic country, too. Where religion loses its hold, where secularism prevails—as it does in most of the Arab world—communism takes hold like a new religion. It is less the believers who turn to communism than the disillusioned ones who seek new solutions. Walt Whitman Rostow's observation is thus correct that "Communism is best understood as a disease of the transition to modernization."[14] The most important phase of this transition, however, is not its economic side, but the spiritual aspect, the mental suffering created by the change-over to a new and sometimes alien civilization.

That poverty breeds communism was accepted as an axiom until R. V. Burks and Giorgio Braga[15] thoroughly disproved this theory. But nationalism is still accepted as something ordained by fate—like the plague in the Middle Ages. Empirically—because no serious sociological research on this problem is known to this writer —one finds, however, many indications that the same conditions, the same individual, social, and political tensions which drive certain people into communism's arms also breed nationalist extremists. Personal and social complexes and tensions are transferred into rebellion against authority. The number of new nations which could be created by restless men is indefinite. Under certain conditions these tensions are channeled into the Communist mold, under certain others—especially when the domination is felt as ethnically alien—into a nationalist form. Where ideology has not yet fastened a firm grip on agitated men, a change-over from communism to nationalism or vice versa poses few problems. This would explain some of the sudden changes which puzzle and confound Western observers in Asia and in Africa: one day a Communist, the next a nationalist, or the other way around. The danger remains that nationalism, which now has the upper hand, may collapse and leave a heap of disappointments and unfulfilled expectations and thus give full rein to communism.

Notes

Chapter I

1. Michel de Montaigne, *Essais* (Paris: Bibliothèque de la Pléiade, 1946), Livre I, Chapitre XXXI (Des cannibales), p. 213.
2. "As lately as the sixteenth century, Islam inspired the same hysteria in Western hearts as communism in the twentieth century, and this essentially for the same reasons. Like communism, Islam was an anti-Western movement which was at the same time a heretical version of a Western faith; and like communism, it wielded a sword of the spirit against which there was no defence in material armaments." Arnold J. Toynbee, *Civilization on Trial* (New York: Oxford University Press, 1948), p. 21 ff.
3. Hermann Alexander, Graf von Keyserling, *Das Reisetagebuch eines Philosophen* (8th ed. Stuttgart-Berlin: Deutsche Verlags-Anstalt, 1932).
4. To a modern American writer, Vance Bourjaily, *The End of My Life* (New York: Bantam Books, 1962), p. 6, it appears, "as though there were a general conspiracy in the Middle East to unfamiliarize itself to Western eyes, so as to disguise its poverty."
5. Kateb Yacine, author of *Nedjma*, left Algeria to rejoin the Provisional Government of the Algerian Republic in Tunis. In *La Femme Sauvage*, published by El Moudjahid (June 4, 1961) he propounds a quaint version of the fight for the liberation of Algeria; writing about Westerns in which the Indians always lose, he expounds: "How many times I wanted to yell with the Indians and fall myself under the white horses! . . . The war of the Algerians has revenged America, the real one, the one of the Indian ancestors!"
6. Mouloud Feraoun, author of *Le fils du pauvre* and other extraordinary works whose locales are usually his native Kabylia, was murdered by

gunmen of the white Organisation Armee Secrète (OAS) underground movement in the spring of 1962. In *Les Poèmes de Si Mohand* (Paris: Les Editions de Minuit, 1960), one of the first books ever published in the Kabyle language rendered in the Latin alphabet and translated into French by Mouloud Feraoun, the Berber bard, Si Mohand, expresses among other things his dislike for all Semites, Arabs, and Jews alike:

> Je jure de rompre avec ces chiens
> Car la confiance a disparu
> En cette génération impie.
>
> Ceux qui avaient mon amitié
> et me payaient de retour
> Aujourd'hui se moquent de moi.
> O coeur, cesse de t'humilier,
> Détourne-toi de l'Arabe
> et des Juifs tant qu'ils sont.

7. "The Sparrow Shall Fall," *The New Yorker*, October 10, 1959. One might add that it is not too difficult to encounter "oriental minds" with different layers of behavior, like onions, in the Western world. . . .

8. Abbé Sieyès, *Qu'est-ce que le Tiers-Etat?* (3rd ed., Paris, 1789), p. 83 ff.

9. Jacques Berque, *Les Arabes d'hier à demain* (Paris: Editions du Seuil, 1960), p. 97.

10. Arnold J. Toynbee, *op. cit.*, p. 23.

11. Luis Diez del Corral, *The Rape of Europe* (London: George Allen & Unwin, 1959), p. 291.

12. The Edwardian picture of a simple contrast between pashas and effendis, described, appropriately, in terms borrowed from the long defunct Ottoman Empire, still turns up from time to time in present-day English literature.

13. Luis Diez del Corral, *op. cit.*, p. 300.

14. Muhsin Mahdi, *Ibn Khaldun's Philosophy of History* (London: Allen & Unwin, 1957), p. 246 ff.

15. Cit. after Jamal Mohammed Ahmed, *The Intellectual Origins of Egyptian Nationalism* (London: Oxford University Press, 1960), p. 8.

16. Luis Diez del Corral, *op. cit.*, p. 222.

17. Jacques Berque, *op. cit.*, p. 25.

18. Malek Bennabi, *Vocation de l'Islam* (Paris: Editions du Seuil, 1959), p. 74 ff.

Chapter II

1. Abdel Khalek Hassouna, *Le nationalisme arabe* (Genève: Centre d' information arabe, 1960), p. 10 f.

2. Philip K. Hitti, *Lebanon in History* (London: Macmillan & Co., 1957), p. 235.

3. "Le Coran est un livre céleste révélé a Mahomet. C'est un Coran arabe, révélé a un prophete arabe, sur une terre arabe, et transmis par le Prophète aux Arabes qui s'y conformèrent et le conservèrent. Il n'est donc pas étonnant que l'on considère le Coran comme un facteur de la manifestation du nationalisme arabe."
Ali Housni al-Kharboutli, *Le Coran et le Nationalisme Arabe.* "Orient" No. 15, 3e Trimestre 1960, p. 161.

4. "Le Coran a commencé son oeuvre en opérant la fusion des différents dialects primitifs; il unit ensuite les coeurs dans le cadre d'une seule religion; enfin il donna aux Arabes la possibilité de rapprocher les langues des autres peuples et les sentiments de leurs coeurs."
Ali Housni al-Kharboutli, *op. cit.*, p. 164.

5. Hazem Zaki Nuseibeh, *The Ideas of Arab Nationalism* (Ithaca: Cornell University Press, 1956), p. 19 ff.

6. "Il trionfo [della lingua araba] significa molto più che la sostituzione di uno a un altro strumento meccanico: esso implica la supremazia, o meglio il dominio assoluto di un atteggiamento psichico e di un tipo d'arte nettamente individuati." Giorgio Levi della Vida, *Aneddoti e svaghi arabi e non arabi* (Milano-Napoli: Riccardo Ricciardi, 1959), p. 9. "The triumph [of the Arabic language] means much more than the substitution of one mechanical instrument by another; it implies the supremacy, or better, the absolute rule of a psychological attitude and of a clearly distinct type of art."

7. H. A. R. Gibb, *Modern Trends in Islam* (3rd Imp. Chicago: The University of Chicago Press, 1954), p. 5.

8. Edward Atiyah, *The Arabs* (A Pelican Book, 1955), p. 96.

9. A discussion this author had in Beirut with Clovis Maqsoud, a widely read political writer, may exemplify the different set of values. Criticizing the author's views on Arab nationalism, but agreeing emphatically that his facts were right, the Western-educated Clovis Maqsoud affirmed: "For you facts are something static, facts are God. For us facts are subjective, something fluid; they change."

10. Wilfred Cantwell Smith, *Islam in Modern History* (New York: Mentor Books, 1959), p. 37.

11. Zeine N. Zeine, *Arab-Turkish Relations and the Emergence of Arab Nationalism* (Beirut-London: Khayat's, 1958), p. 24. Omar Khayyam formulates the same idea in one of his poems:

> See, how upon the Slate of Doom
> Our Master, from eternity,

Inscribed the sum of all to be
And for revision left no room.
—*Omar Khayyam,* by Arthur J. Arberry
(London: John Murray, 1952), p. 139.

12. H. A. R. Gibb, *op. cit.,* p. 87 ff.
13. Quoted after Edward Atiyah, *The Arabs,* p. 46, who adds: "Ibn Khaldun here was using the word *Arab* to designate the Bedouin tribes of the Arabian Peninsula, but it is certainly open to question whether the extreme and turbulent individualism of the desert inhabitants did not, despite the discipline of Islam, impart strong centrifugal tendencies to the whole Arab Empire, and remain the basic social weakness of Arabs even after centuries of settled life in fusion with other races."
14. Hazem Zaki Nuseibeh, *op. cit.,* p. 8.
15. Gamal Abdel Nasser, *The Philosophy of the Revolution* (Cairo: Mondiale Press, n.d.), p. 21.
16. H. A. R. Gibb, *Mohammedanism* (New York: Mentor Books, 1955), p. 17.
17. G. E. von Grunebaum, "Islam: its inherent power of expansion and adaptation," *City Invincible* (Chicago: University of Chicago Press, 1960), p. 444 ff. and *"Modern Islam"* (Berkeley and Los Angeles: University of California Press, 1962), p. 8 f.
18. Joseph F. Schacht, "The Islamic Background of the Idea of an Arab Nation," *The Arab Nation* (Washington: The Middle East Institute, 1960), p. 21.
19. Hazem Zaki Nuseibeh, *op. cit.,* p. 12.
20. *Ibid.,* p. 24, p. 32 f.
21. *Ibid.,* p. 47.
22. Joseph F. Schacht, "The Islamic Background of the Idea of an Arab Nation," *The Arab Nation* (Washington, D.C.: The Middle East Institute, 1960), p. 21.
23. Abdul Rahman Azzam, *op. cit.,* p. 5 ff. See also: "The Myth of the Fourteenth Muslim Century" in George E. Kirk, *Contemporary Arab Politics* (New York: Frederick A. Praeger, 1961).
24. Friedrich-Wilhelm Fernau, *Arabischer Westen* (Stuttgart: Curt E. Schwab, 1959), p. 116.
25. Wilfred Cantwell Smith, *op. cit.,* p. 63.
26. *Ibid.,* p. 47 ff.
27. Ziya Gökalp, *Turkish Nationalism and Western Civilization.* Trans. by Niyazi Berkes (London: Allen and Unwin, Ltd., 1959), p. 76, p. 127.
28. Wilfred Cantwell Smith, *op. cit.,* p. 85.
29. Hazem Zaki Nuseibeh, *op. cit.,* p. 29.
30. Georges Hanna, "Le sens du nationalisme arabe," quoted in "Orient" No. 18, p. 185 (Paris 1961).

31. Marouf al-Dawalibi, "La verité sur le nationalisme arabe," *Orient* cit., p. 184 f.
32. Philip K. Hitti, *Lebanon in History*, p. 478 ff.
33. Wilfred Cantwell Smith, *op. cit.*, p. 83, p. 99.
34. Hazem Zaki Nuseibeh, *op. cit.*, p. 53.
35. *Ibid.*, p. 68.
36. *Ibid.*, p. 91, p. 93.
37. Muhammad Abdallah al-Arabi, *The Democracy of Arab Nationalism between Communist Democracy and Capitalist Democracy*. See Fahim I. Qubain, *Inside the Arab Mind* (Washington, 1960), p. 1.
38. Jacques Austruy, *L'Islam face au développement économique* (Paris: Les Editions Ouvrières, 1961), p. 116 f.
39. S. H. Al-Shamma, *The Ethical System Underlying the Qur'an* (Thesis presented to the University of Edinburgh [Tübingen: Hopfer-Verlag, 1959]), p. 110, p. 119 f.
40. Arnold Toynbee, "The Future Religion of Africa," *New York Herald Tribune*, European edition, Jan. 14-15, 1961. Reprinted from Observer Foreign News Service (OFNS).
41. Arnold Toynbee, OFNS No. 17198, London, August 2, 1961.
42. *New York Herald Tribune, op. cit.*, Jan. 14-15, 1961.
43. See for exemplars: Anwar G. Chejne, "The Use of History by Modern Arab Writers," *The Middle East Journal*, Autumn 1960, p. 394 ff.
44. *El Moudjahid*, February 1, 1958.
45. *El Moudjahid*, September 29, 1959.
46. Ziya Gökalp, *op. cit.*, p 80 f.
47. Zeine N. Zeine, *op. cit.*, p. 117 ff.
48. Gamal Abdel Nasser, *The Philosophy of the Revolution*, p. 71 f.
49. *Ibid.*, p. 54.
50. *Ibid.*, p. 53, p. 70.
51. *Ibid.*, p. 71.
52. Zeine N. Zeine, *op cit.*, p. 118, p. 122 f.
53. *The New York Times*, June 5, 1962. Report by Dana Adams Schmidt from Beirut.
54. See the excellent book of Ishak Musa Husaini, *The Moslem Brethren* (Beirut: Khayat's, 1956).
55. See Fahim I. Qubain, *Inside the Arab Mind* (Arlington, Va.: Middle East Research Associates, 1960), p. 23 ff.
56. Philip K. Hitti, *op. cit.*, p. 241, p. 256.
57. Wilfred Cantwell Smith, *op. cit.*, p. 86.
58. Sylvia Haim, *Arab Nationalism* (Berkeley and Los Angeles: University of California Press, 1962), p. 57 ff.
59. Philip K. Hitti, *op. cit.*, p. 480.
60. Wilfred Cantwell Smith, *op. cit.*, p. 57.
61. G. E. von Grunebaum, *Islam—Expansion and Adaptation* in *City In-*

vincible (Chicago: University of Chicago Press, 1960), p. 446 ff.

62. *Orient* No. 16, 4e Trimestre, 1960.
63. Wilfred Cantwell Smith, *op. cit.*, p. 82.
64. *Ibid.*, p. 83, p. 113.
65. Hazem Zaki Nuseibeh, *op. cit.*, p. 45.
66. H. A. R. Gibb, *Modern Trends in Islam*, p. 50 f.

Chapter III

1. Huxley, Julian S., & Haddon, A. C., *We Europeans* (Oxford: Clarendon Press, 1940).
2. Fayez Sayegh, *Arab Unity* (New York: Devin-Adair, 1958), p. 214.
3. Hans E. Tütsch: *Die Repräsentation in der Demokratie.* (Zürich 1944), p. 52 f.
4. The expression "territorial state," derived from the German *Territorial-staat*, is now also used by American historians (see William J. Bossen-brook, *The German Mind* (Detroit: Wayne State University Press, 1961), because it cannot create misunderstandings like the more common term "national state," which is used for two different historical phenomena. The formation of a "territorial state," concentrating all authority in the hands of a central government while curtailing the personal power of feudal lords, obviously differs from the creation of "national states" in the 19th and 20th centuries.
5. Lowell Thomas, *With Lawrence in Arabia* (New York: Popular Library Edition, 1961), p. 223.
6. In an interview with the writer.
7. Abdel Khalek Hassouna, *L'activité de la Ligue des Etats arabes* (Genève: Centre d'information arabe, 1960), p. 6.
8. The name of the leader of the Kataeb is spelled here the way he himself transcribes it. Not wanting to be more Arab than an Arab, this writer rejects the transcription Jumayyil found in many English language books. The same principle is applied in other cases: since the Egyptian information services transcribe the name of their supreme chief Gamal Abdel Nasser, we do not spell it Jamal Abd an-Nassir. Bourguiba is not arabized into Abu Raqiba.
9. See Arnold Hottinger, "Nassers Schatten über Syrien," *Neue Zürcher Zeitung*, April 25, 1962.
10. Which reminds us of an electoral campaign in Sicily where the speaker of the day, haranguing the people in the hot and dusty village square, promises a new school, a new municipal building, a new bridge. . . . Whereon a heckler shouts: "We have no river to build a bridge over." And the speaker rejoins unshaken: "You shall also get a river. . . ."
11. Gamal Abdel Nasser, *The Philosophy of the Revolution*, p. 38.
12. *Ibid.*, p. 20.

13. Published by the Départment de l'Information of the United Arab Republic (Cairo, n.d. [May or June, 1962]), p. 17, p. 23.
14. *Ibid.*, p. 117.
15. *Ibid.*, p. 118 ff.
16. *Ibid.*, p. 121.
17. *New York Times*, International Edition, May 11, 1964.
18. *New York Times*, International Edition, May 18, 1964.
19. "Die deutsche Frau schminkt sich nicht," was a well-known Goebbels slogan.
20. Lord Acton, *Lectures on Modern History* (London: The Fontana Library, 1960), p. 77.
21. "Dokumente über die Selbstverwaltung." Published by the Ministry of Information of the "Algerische Demokratische Volksrepublik." Bône, n.d.
22. *Constitution de la République Algérienne Democratique et Populaire.* Published by the "Bureau Politique." No place, no date.
23. Avant-Projet du Programme du Parti FLN. *Révolution africaine,* April 11, 1964, No. 63.
    Amendments accepted by the party congress. *Alger républicain,* April 22, 1964.
24. Opening speech of Ben Bella to the party congress. *Révolution africaine,* April 18, 1964, No. 64.
25. Translations by Leonard Binder in the *Middle East Journal,* (Spring, 1959) and by Sylvia G. Haim in *Arab Nationalism* (University of California Press, 1962).
26. See the declaration of the Baath party of May, 1962. *Neue Zürcher Zeitung,* Fernausgabe (foreign edition), May 29, 1962, Nr. 156.
27. E. H. Saab, *Jeune Afrique*, July 27, 1964, No. 194.

Chapter IV

1. William, J. Bossenbrook, *The German Mind*, (Detroit: Wayne State University Press, 1962), p. 368.
2. In a talk with the author in December, 1960.
3. Sati al-Husri, *Arabism First* (Beirut: Dar al-Ilm, 1958)
4. Zeine N. Zeine, *op. cit.*, p. 127.
5. "A common past, except for folk song and legend, is chiefly the possession of but the literate individuals in any nation," Boyd C. Shafer, *Nationalism—Myth and Reality* (New York: Harcourt, Brace, & World, 1955), p. 56.
6. Jacques Berque: *Les Arabes d'hier à demain* (Paris: Editions du Seuil 1960), p. 42.
7. Jacques Berque, *op. cit.*, p. 188, p. 191.
8. Malek Bennabi, *Vocation de l'Islam* (Paris: Editions du Seuil, 1954), p. 154.

9. Khrushchev's visit in Egypt in 1964 brought again a change in the party line. Khaled Bagdash, the Kurdish leader of the Syrian communists, on September 8, 1964, interpreted the new course in the French communist newspaper "L'Humanité" authoritatively: "The idea of unity grows from objective conditions: the common history, the common language, and the geographical position of the Arab countries." Unity, according to Bagdash, should be based on the interests of the masses, the workers, and it should take into account the differences between each country.

10. Beirut: Editions de la Revue Phénicienne, 1934.

11. Anwar G. Chejne, "Egyptian Attitudes toward Pan-Arabism" *The Middle East Journal*, Summer, 1957.

12. According to a Reuter dispatch from Baghdad reprinted in the *New York Times* of June 16, 1962.

13. For a more detailed report on Arab-Israeli relations *see* Hans E. Tütsch, *Die arabischen Völker am Kreuzweg* (Zürich, 1956).

14. *The New York Times* Magazine, July 8, 1962.

15. R. V. Burks, *The Dynamics of Communism in Eastern Europe* (Princeton University Press, 1961).

Giorgio Braga, *Il comunismo fra gli italiani* (Milano: Comunità, 1959).

Bibliography

Ahmed, Jamal Mohammed. *The Intellectual Origins of Egyptian National-ism.* London and New York: Oxford University Press, 1960.

Aït Ahmed, Hocine. *La Guerre et l'Après-Guerre.* Paris: Les Editions de Minuit, 1964.

"The Algerian Constitution," *Middle East Journal* (Autumn, 1963).

Antonious, George. *The Arab Awakening.* Beirut: Khayat's, 1938.

The Arab Nation: Addresses presented at the fourteenth annual conference. Washington, D.C.: The Middle East Institute, 1960.

Atiyah, Edward. *The Arabs.* (A Pelican Book) Harmondsworth, Middlesex: Penguin Books, Ltd., 1955.

Barbour, Nevill. *A Survey of North West Africa (The Mahgrib).* London and New York: Oxford University Press, 1959.

Baulin, Jacques. *The Arab Role in Africa.* Harmondsworth, Middlesex: Penguin African Library, 1962.

Beling, Willard A. *Pan-Arabism and Labour.* Cambridge: Harvard University Press, 1960.

Ben Barka, Mehdi. *Problèmes d'édification du Maroc et du Maghreb.* Quatre entretiens avec El-Mehdi ben Barka, recueuillis par Raymond Jean. Paris: Plon, 1959.

Bennabi, Malek. *Vocation de l'Islam.* Paris: Editions du Seuil, 1954.

———. *L'Afro-Asiatisme.* Cairo: Imprimerie Misr, 1956.

Berniard, Stéphane. *Maroc 1943-1956.* Editions de l'Institut de Sociologie de l'Université Libre de Bruxelles. 3 vols. 1963.

Berque, Jacques. *Les Arabes d'hier à demain.* Paris: Editions du Seuil, 1960.

———. *Les Arabes.* Paris: Robert Delpire Editeur, 1959.

Bonn, Gisela. *Das doppelte Gesicht des Sudan.* Wiesbaden: F. A. Brockhaus, 1961.

147

Bossenbrook, William J. *The German Mind.* Detroit: Wayne State University Press, 1961.

Boudiaf, Mohared. *Où va l'Algérie?* Paris: Librairie de l'Etoile, 1964.

Bourdieu, Pierre. *Sociologie de l'Algérie.* Paris: Ed. "Que sais-je?", 1958.

Bourdieu, Pierre; Darbel, Alain; Rivet, Jean-Paul; et Seibel, Claude. *Travail et Travailleurs en Algérie.* Paris et La Haye: Mouton & Co., 1963.

Bourdieu, Pierre et Sayad, Abdelmalek. *Le Déracinement.* Paris: Les Editions de Minuit, 1964.

Bourguiba, Habib. *La Tunisie et la France.* Paris: Juillard, 1954.

Braga, Giorgio. *Il comunismo fra gli italiani.* Milano: Comunità, 1956.

Bretholz, Wolfgang. *Aufstand der Araber.* München: Verlag Kurt Desch, 1960.

Brockelmann, Carl. *History of the Islamic Peoples.* New York: Capricorn Book, 1960.

Bromberger, Merry et Serge. *Les 13 complots du 13 mai.* Paris: A. Fayard, 1959.

Burks, R. V. *The Dynamics of Communism in Eastern Europe.* Princeton: Princeton University Press, 1961.

Campbell, John C. *Defense of the Middle East.* Rev. ed., New York: Frederick A. Praeger, 1961.

Chamoun, Camille. *Crise au Moyen-Orient.* Paris: Gallimard, 1963.

Chejne, Anwar G. "The Use of History by Modern Arab Writers," *Middle East Journal* (Autumn, 1960).

————. "Egyptian Attitudes toward Pan-Arabism," *Middle East Journal* (Summer, 1957).

Clark, Michael K. *Algeria in Turmoil.* London: Thames and Hudson, 1960.

Corral, Luis Diez del. *The Rape of Europe.* London: Allen & Unwin, 1959.

Dean, Vera Micheles. *The Nature of the Non-Western World.* New York: A Mentor Book, 1957.

Duquesne, Jacques. *L'Algérie ou la guerre des mythes.* Bruges: Desclée De Brouwer, 1958.

Ellis, Harry B. *Challenge in the Middle East.* New York: Ronald Press, 1961.

Faris, N. A., and Husayn, M. T. *The Crescent in Crisis.* University of Kansas Press, 1955.

al-Fasi, Alal. *The Independence Movements in Arab North Africa.* Washington, D.C.: American Council of Learned Societies, 1954.

Fernau, Friedrich-Wilhelm. *Arabischer Westen.* Stuttgart: Verlag Curt E. Schwab, 1959.

————. *Flackernder Halbmond.* Eugen Rentsch-Verlag, Erlenbach-Zürich, 1953. English ed. *Moslems on the March.* New York: Knopf, 1954.

Gabrieli, Francesco. *Il risorgimento arabo.* Torino: Giulio Einaudi, 1958. English ed. *The Arab Revival.* New York: Random House, 1961.

Gemayel, Pierre. *Connaissance des Kataeb.* Beirut: Imprimérie Jeanne d'Arc, 1948.

Gibb, H. A. R. *Modern Trends in Islam.* Third Impression, Chicago: The University of Chicago Press, 1954.

———. *Mohammedanism.* New York: Mentor Book, 1955.

Godchot, J. E. *Les constitutions du Proche et du Moyen Orient.* Paris: Sirey, 1957.

Gökalp, Ziya. *Turkish Nationalism and Western Civilization.* Translated and edited by Niyazi Berkes. London: Allen & Unwin, 1960.

Grunebaum, G. E. von. *Medieval Islam.* 2nd ed.; Chicago: University of Chicago Press, 1953.

———. *Klassizismus und Kulturzerfall.* Frankfurt am Main: Vittorio Klostermann, 1960.

———. *Islam. Die Entstchung Europas.* Propyläen-Weltgeschichte, Vol. V. Berlin, Frankfurt a/M, Wien: Propyläen-Verlag, 1963.

———. "Islam: Its Inherent Power of Expansion and Adaptation," *City Invincible.* Chicago: University of Chicago Press, 1960.

———. *Modern Islam. The Search for Cultural Identity.* Berkeley and Los Angeles: University of California Press, 1962.

Haim, Sylvia G. *Arab Nationalism: An Anthology.* Berkeley and Los Angeles: University of California Press, 1962.

Hassouna, Abdel Khalek. *L'Activité de la Ligue des Etats arabes. Le nationalisme arabe. L'Islam et l'age atomique.* Genève: Centre d'information arabe, 1960.

Heilperin, M. A. *Le Nationalisme Economique.* Paris: Payot, 1963.

Hitti, Philip K. *The Near East in History.* Princeton: Van Nostrand, 1961.

———. *Lebanon in History.* London: Macmillan & Co., 1957.

Hostler, Charles Warren. *Turkism and the Soviets.* London: Allen & Unwin, 1957.

Hottinger, Arnold. *Die Araber-Werden, Wesen, Wandel und Krise des Arabertums.* Zürich: Atlantis-Verlag, 1960.

———. English editions: *The Arabs.* Berkeley and Los Angeles: University of California Press, 1963. London: Thames and Hudson, 1963.

Hourani, A. H. *Syria and Lebanon.* London and New York: Oxford University Press, 1946.

Husaini, Ishak Musa. *The Moslem Brethren.* Beirut: Khayat's, 1956.

Jaspers, Karl. *Vom Ursprung und Ziel der Geschichte.* München: R. Piper Verlag, 1949.

Jumblat, Kamal. *Démocratic nouvelle.* (n.p., n.d.)

———. *Islam and Communism: A Conference.* New York: Institute for the Study of the USSR, 1960.

Khadduri, Majid. *Independent Iraq.* London and New York: Oxford University Press, 1960.

Khadduri, Majid, and Liebesny, Herbert J. *Law in the Middle East.* Washington: Middle East Institute, 1955.

Kedourie, Elie. *Nationalism.* New York: Frederick A. Praeger, 1960.

Kirk, George E. *A Short History of the Middle East.* 6th Rev. ed., New York: Frederick A. Praeger, 1960.

———. *Contemporary Arab Politics.* New York: Frederick A. Praeger, 1961.

Kohn, Hans. *Nationalism.* (An Anvil Original) New York: Van Nostrand, 1955.

———. *The Idea of Nationalism.* New York: Macmillan, 1944.

———. *Pan-Slavism.* South Bend, Indiana: University of Notre Dame Press, 1953.

———. *Nationalismus und Imperialismus im Vorderen Orient.* Frankfurt am Main: Societäts-Verlag, 1931.

Kraft, Joseph. *The Struggle for Algeria.* New York: Doubleday, 1961.

Lacouture, Jean et Simonne. *Le Maroc à l'épreuve.* Paris: Editions du Seuil, 1958.

———. *Egypt in Transition* (translated from French). New York: Criterion Books, 1958.

Laqueur, Walter. *Communism and Nationalism in the Middle East.* New York: Frederick A. Praeger, 1956.

———. *The Middle East in Transition.* New York: Frederick A. Praeger, 1958.

———. *The Soviet Union and the Middle East.* New York: Frederick A. Praeger, 1959.

Lemberg, Eugen. *Nationalismus.* Reinbek bei Hamburg: Rowohlts Deutsche Enzyklopädie, 1964.

Lenczowski, George. *The Middle East in World Affairs.* Ithaca: Cornell University Press, 1956.

———. *Oil and State in the Middle East.* Ithaca: Cornell University Press, 1960.

Lengyel, Emil. *The Changing Middle East.* New York: The John Day Company, 1960.

Les Etats Arabes. Centre d'Information Arabe de Genève, 1960.

Levi Della Vida, Giorgio. *Aneddoti e svaghi arabi e non arabi.* Milano-Napoli: Riccardo Ricciardi, 1959.

Lewis, Bernard. *The Arabs in History.* London: Hutchinson, Ltd., 1958.

———. *The Middle East and the West.* Bloomington, Indiana: Indiana University Press, 1964.

Little, Tom. *Egypt.* New York: Frederick A. Praeger, 1959.

Longrigg, Stephen and Stoakes, Frank. *Iraq.* New York: Frederick A. Praeger, 1960.

Mahdi, Muhsin. *Ibn Khaldun's Philosophy of History.* London: Allen & Unwin, 1957.

Malek, Anouar Abdel. *Egypte—Société Militaire.* Paris: Editions du Seuil, 1962.

McNeill, William H. *The Rise of the West*. Chicago and London: Chicago University Press, 1963.

Meinecke, Friedrich. *Weltbürgertum und Nationalstaat*. Berlin-München: R. Oldenbourg, 1928.

The Middle East. London: The Royal Institute of International Affairs, 1958.

Monnerot, Jules. *Sociologie du communisme*. Paris: Gallimard, 1949.

Nasser, Gamal Abdel. *The Philosophy of the Revolution*. Cairo: "Mondiale" Press, n.d.

Northrop, F. S. C. *The Meeting of East and West*. New York: Macmillan Paperbacks, 1960.

Nuseibeh, Hazem Zaki. *The Ideas of Arab Nationalism*. Ithaca: Cornell University Press, 1956.

Omodeo, Adolfo. *L'età del Risorgimento italiano*. 5th ed., Napoli: "Esi," 1947.

Patai, Raphael. *The Kingdom of Jordan*. Princeton: Princeton University Press, 1958.

Qubain, Fahim I. *Inside the Arab Mind*. (A bibliographical survey) Arlington, Virginia: Middle East Research Associates, 1960.

Rondot, Pierre. *The Changing Patterns of the Middle East*. New York: Frederick A. Praeger, 1961.

Saab, Hassan. *Arab Federalism*. The Middle East Forum (November-December, 1958).

Sadat, Anwar. *Revolt on the Nile*. New York: The John Day Company, 1957.

Sayegh, Fayez A. *Arab Unity: Hope and Fulfillment*. New York: Devin-Adair, 1958.

Schaeder, Hans Heinrich. *Der Mensch in Orient und Okzident*. München: R. Piper-Verlag, 1960.

Scheler, Max. *Nation und Weltanschauung*. Leipzig: Der neue Geist Verlag, 1923.

Schmidt, Dana Adams. *Journey Among Brave Men*. Boston and Toronto: Little, Brown and Company, 1964.

Shafer, Boyd C. *Nationalism—Myth and Reality*. New York: Harcourt, Brace & World, 1955.

Shwadran, Benjamin. *The Power Struggle in Iraq*. New York: Council for Middle Eastern Affairs Press, 1960.

Smith, Wilfred Cantwell. *Islam in Modern History*. New York: Mentor Books, 1959.

Tarn, W. W. *Hellenistic Civilisation*. Rev. ed. New York: Meridian Book, 1961.

Thayer, Charles W. *Diplomat*. New York: Harper & Brothers, 1959.

Toynbee, Arnold J. *Civilization on Trial*. New York: Oxford University Press, 1948.

Tütsch, Hans E. *Die arabischen Völker am Kreuzweg.* Zürich: Buchverlag der Neuen Zürcher Zeitung, 1956.

———. *Vorderasien in Aufruhr.* Zürich: Buchverlag der NZZ, 1959.

———. *Nordafrika in Gärung.* Zürich: Buchverlag der NZZ, 1960.

———. *Die Repräsentation in der Demokratie.* Dissertation, Zürich, 1944.

———. *From Ankara to Marrakesh.* London: George Allen and Unwin, 1964.

Villard, Henry S. *Libya.* Ithaca: Cornell University Press, 1956.

Warriner, Doreen. *Land Reform and Development in the Middle East.* London: The Royal Institute of International Affairs, 1957.

Weulersse, Jacques. *Paysans de Syrie et du Proche Orient.* Paris: Gallimard, 1946.

Wheelock, Keith. *Nasser's New Egypt.* New York: Frederick A. Praeger, 1960.

Zeine, Zeine N. *Arab-Turkish Relations and the Emergence of Arab Nationalism.* Beirut-London: Khayat's, 1958.

Ziegler, Heinz O. *Die moderne Nation.* Tübingen: Mohr, 1931.

For a bibliography of articles and books about Arab nationalism and especially for short summaries of Arab opinions *see*

Fahim I. Qubain. *Inside the Arab Mind.*

Sylvia Haim in *Arab Nationalism* gives translations of important Arab writings on nationalism.

Index

Abbas, Ferhat, 131
Abbassid Empire, 58
Abduh, Muhammad, 65, 68, 122
Abdullah, Emir, 125
Afghani, Jamal ed-Din. *See* Jamal
 ed-Din al-Afghani
Aflaq, Michel, 50, 102, 103
al-Afghani, Jamal ed-Din, 65, 68
al-Arabi, Muhammad Abdallah, 51
al-Azmah, Bashir, 126
al-Banna, Hassan, 61-62
Al-bilad as-sudan, 127
Algeria: formation of, 56; co-operation with Egypt, 123
Algerian Muslims, 56
Algerian National Liberation Front,
 62; newspaper of, 56
Algerian Socialism, 98-106
al-Ghazali, Muhammad, 98
Ali, Muhammad, 122
al-Kawakibi, Abdel Rahman, 65
al-Khuri, Beshara, 120
al-Kuwatly, Shukry, 86
al-Maani, Fahreddin, 121
al-Madani, Tewfik, 62
al-Majali, Hazzaa, 85
al-Mutawakkil, Caliph, 66

al-Nabhini, Takieddin, 62
al-Qudsi, Nazim, 122-123
Amer, Abdul Hakim, 102
Arab: defined, 32; history, 43-46
Arabian Peninsula, 125, 126-127
Arabi, Muhammad Abdallah. *See*
 Muhammad Abdallah al-Arabi
Arabic, 35-37
Arab imperialism, 128-132
Arab law, 37-43
Arab nationalism: Christian Arabs'
 attitude, 51; history of, 53-54;
 mutations of, 53-58; birth of, 60;
 dissensions, 21, 109-110; non-
 Muslim dissidents, 111-112; Mid-
 dle Eastern Christian attitude
 toward, 67; impediments to,
 124; contribution of Zionism,
 132-133; dangers of, 138. *See*
 also Local nationalism, Regional
 nationalism
"Arab socialism": Nasser's attempt
 to justify, 60
Arab-Turkish relations, 57-58
Arab unity: obstructions to, 41-42;
 power of language, 115-116

Arab world: problems of, 83-87; attitude toward U.S. military, 117-118
Arabism: defined, 70
Arabs: anti-Western sentiment, 64-65
Arslan, Emir Majid, 120
as-Sadat, Anwar, 58, 88-89, 129-130
as-Said, Nuri, 125
Association of the Ulemas, 62, 64
Azmah, Bashir. *See* Bashir al-Azmah
Azzam, Abdul Rahman, 55

Baath party, 101-106, 118, 136
Baathists. *See* Baath party
Balfour Doctrine, 132
Banna, Hassan. *See* Hassan al-Banna
Ben Bella, Ahmed: Algerian socialism, 99-100, 101, 111
Beirut, 121
Berbers, 35
Bizerte, 130
Bourguiba, Habib, 61, 128, 130

Charter of Addis Ababa, 132
Charter of Arab Socialism, 97
Chamoun, Camille, 120
Chehab, Fuad, 84
Christians: attitude toward Pan-Arab nationalism, 111; Middle Eastern attitudes toward Arab nationalism, 66-67
Colonialism, 70-71, 84-85
Communism: obstacles to acceptance of, 134-137; methods of infiltration, 136-138; approaches, 137-138; China-Soviet competition, 135
Communist party, 63; attitude toward Pan-Arab nationalism, 118; banned, 136-137
Council of the Revolution, 123
Cyprus, 129-130

Damascenes, 130
Dar al-Islam, 133

Druses, 120

Egypt: history of nationalism, 122-123; co-operation with Tunisia, 123-124
es-Solh, Riad, 120
es-Solh, Sami, 120

Faisal, Emir, 126
Fertile Crescent, 125-126
Free Officers of Muhammad Nagib and Gamal Abdel Nasser, 62

Ghazali, Muhammad, *See* Muhammad al-Ghazali
Gökalp, Ziya, 56-57
Greater Syria, 126
Greater Syria Party. *See* Popular Socialist party
Guedira, Ahmed Reda, 99

Haraka Chaabia, 127
Hashemites, 54, 125
Hassan II, King: role in Morocco dispute, 131
Hassouna, Abdel Khalek, 87-90 *passim*
Haurani, Akram, 105
Hussain, Sherif, 58
Hussein, King, 61, 62, 84, 127

ibn Saud, Abdul Aziz, 126
Iraq: claim to Kuwait, 130
Iraqi Communists, 135
Iraqi Muslim party, 63-64, 66
Istiqlal party, 127
Islam: development of, 32-35; spiritual crisis, 46; role it plays in Arab nationalism, 51, 55; source of Arab unity, 58; as a political force, 58; power today, 65-66; attitude toward minority groups, 66-67; relation to Pan-Arabism, 68; reform movement, 68-70; appeal to modernize, 69; intel-

Islam—*Cont.*
lectual attitude toward, 70;
masses' view toward, 70; secular
aspect of, 70-73; schism between
Sunnites and Shiites, 110-111;
decay of rules, 113; decay of
law, 113-114; effect of Western
technology, 115; creed, 129
Islamic Conference, 61
Islamic Congress, 58-59
Islamic parties: Muslim brotherhood,
61-62; Free Officers of Muhammad Nagib and Gamal Abdel
Nasser, 62; Association of the
Ulemas, 62; Liberation (Tahrir)
party of Sheikh Takieddin al-
Nabhini, 62-63, 64; Iraqi Muslim party, 63-64; power of, 64
Islamic World Center, the, 60
Israel: Iraqi Muslim party solution
to, 63; Pan-Arab hostility to,
79-80; Western support, 132-133;
Arab solution to, 133

Jordon, 119, 130
Jumblat, Kamal, 99, 103, 120

Kassem, Abdul Karim, 63, 64; atti-
tude toward Arab unity, 118;
Fertile Crescent, 126; claim to
Kuwait, 130
Kawakibi, Abdel Rahman. *See*
Abdel Rahman al-Kawakibi
Khan, Ayub, 69
Khrushchev, Nikita, 117; attitude
toward the Arab world, 134-135
Khuri, Beshara. *See* Beshara al-Khuri
Koran: basis for Muslim law, 37-38;
Nasser's use of, 60; Iraqi Mus-
lim party use of, 63
Kurdish Democratic party, 136
Kurds: Muslim, 130
Kuwait, 119
Kuwatly, Shukry. *See* Shukry al-
Kuwatly

League of Arab States, 82, 87-90, 123
"League of the Islamic World," 61
Lebanese civil war, 126
Lebanon, 121-122; attitude toward
Islam, 65; variations of national-
istic attitudes, 67-68; attempt at
Arab unity, 117; as representa-
tive of Arab spectrum, 119-121
Liberation (Tahrir) party, 64-65, 66
Libya, 123
Local nationalism, 54, 116-124

Maani, Fahreddin. *See* Fahreddin
al-Maani
Madani, Tewfik. *See* Tewfik al-
Madani
Maghreb, 123, 125, 127
Maghreb Federation, 127-128
Maghrebian nationalism, 56
Majali, Hazzaa. *See* Hazzaa al-
Majali
Mandate Territory of Palestine, 132
Maraboutism, 111
Maronite Christians, 120, 129
Mauretania: claims in North Africa,
130, 132
Meouchi, 120
Mesopotamia, 135-136
millet system, 38-39, 47-48, 111
Mohammed, Sultan, 131
Morocco, 124; claims in North
Africa, 130-132
Muslim Africa, 59
Muslim Brotherhood, 61-62, 64
Muslims: in Cyprus, 129-130
Mutawakkil, Caliph. *See* Caliph al-
Mutawakkil

Nabhini, Takieddin. *See* Takieddin
al-Nabhini
Nasser, Gamal Abdel: disgust with
Arab egotism, 41-42; interest in
Muslim Africa, 59; belief in
Islam, 59-60; exploits Pan-Islam-
ism, 60; as seen by the West-

Nasser, Gamal Abdel—*Cont.*
erner, 90; as seen by the Arab, 90-91; his main weapon, 91; necessity of revolution, 93; on Arab unity, 93-94; socialist ambitions, 94; endangers Arab unity, 95; treatment of Syria, 95; one-sided neutralism, 96; economic aims, 97; advantages, 97-98; support from the West, 98; treatment of Baath party, 102; Pan-Arab nationalism, 123; reaction to Israel, 132-133; attitude toward communism, 137; mentioned, 51, 58, 60, 82, 126, 143

Nasserism, 90-98
National Convenant, 120
National Liberation Front of Algeria, 123-24, 127, 136
National Union of Popular Forces, 99
Nationalism: difficulty of co-ordination with religion, 54-55; relationship to religion, 55-56; historic roots, 55-57; intellectual attitude toward, 77; masses' attitude toward, 77
Neodestour party, 127, 136
Nile Valley, 135; unity of, 127
North Africa: regional unification, 127; boundary problems, 130-132; attitude toward Israel, 133

Organization of African Unity: role in Morocco-Algeria dispute, 131
Ottoman Empire, 45, 54, 57, 58, 83-84, 120, 122

Pan-Arabism: composed of, 53; link to Pan-Islamism, 63; necessity of Islam, 68; disparity between ideal and reality, 82
Pan-Arab Nationalism: history of, 54; as one form of Arab nationalism, 77-78; methods of, 78; unified by, 79-80; consequences of desire for unity, 80, 86-87; definition of a nation, 82-83; rejects foreign-drawn borders, 86; appeal of Bedouin mentality, 86; division over achieving unity, 87-89; effect on Asian Arab countries, 116-117; Communist party attitude toward, 118; conflict with Lebanese nationalism, 120-121; resistance from local nationalism, 121-122; strengthened by Israel, 132-133

Pan-Islamism, 53; as political force, 58; exploited by Nasser, 60
"pan" movements: history of, 78-80
Pan-Turkism, 79
Popular Socialist party, 120-121, 125-126, 129
Provisional Government of Algerian Republic, 131

Qudsi, Nazim. *See* Nazim al-Qudsi
"Qudsi Plan," 122-123

Regional nationalism, 124-128
Rimawi, Abdallah, 105

Saadeh, Antun, party of, 99, 126
Sabban, Muhammad Surur, 61
Sadat, Anwar. *See* Anwar as-Sadat
Said, Nuri. *See* Nuri as-Said
Sarraj, Abdul Hamid, 102, 126
Saud, Abdul Aziz. *See* Abdul Aziz ibn Saud
Saudi Arabia, 119
Secularism, 112-113; effect on Islam, 114; breeding-ground for communism, 137
Secularization. *See* Secularism
Shehab, Beahir, 121
Shehab, Fuad, 120
Sherifiau Kingdom, 130
Shiites, 110-111; in Lebanon, 120-121

Solh, Riad. *See* Riad es-Solh
Solh, Sami. See Sami es-Sohl
Sudan, 119, 127
Sunnites, 110-111; in Lebanon, 120-121
Syria: secession from United Arab Republic, 102; loss of influence, 118-119
Syro-Lebanese party, 118

Tunisia: secularism, 112, 123
Turkey: result of secularization, 71-72; as a democracy, 80-81; secularism, 112-113
Turkish-Arab relations, 57-58

umma: defined, 47
Union of Popular Forces, 136
United Arab States, 117
United Arab Republic: socialist charter for, 93; responsibility of, 94
United Nations, 118

Universalism, 47-49

Wafd, 122
Western civilization: dichotomy of acceptance and rejection of, 81-82
Western law: replaces Islamic law, 113-114
Western technology: Arab attitude toward, 15-16, 20, 26-27; effect on Arab manufacturing, 16-17; responsible for ethnic decay, 17-18, 22-23; colonialism, 21-22; slow Arab adaptation to, 23-25; effect on Arab law, domestic, 24; effect on Arab law, religious, 25; effect on Islam, 115; Arabs impressed by, 117

Yemen, 119

Zaghlul, Saad, 122
Zuraiq, Questantin, 67

The manuscript was edited by Elvin T. Gidley and the book was designed by Richard Kinney. The text typefaces are Linotype Granjon originally cut by Claude Garamond but redesigned by George W. Jones. The display typeface is Legend designed by F. H. E. Schneidler in 1937 for Bauer.

The book is printed on Allied Paper Company's Paperback Offset Paper and the paper edition is bound in Reigel Carolina Coated Cover. The hard cover edition is bound in Joanna Mills Parchment cloth. Manufactured in the United States of America.